THE 100 GREATEST CAJUN RECIPES

OTHER BOOKS BY JUDE W. THERIOT, CCP

La Meilleure de la Louisiane (1980)

La Cuisine Cajun (1986)

New American Light Cuisine (1988)

Cajun Quick (1992)

Cajun Healthy (1994)

Cajun Low Carb (2005)

THE 100 GREATEST CAJUN RECIPES

JUDE W. THERIOT, CCP

Pelican Publishing Company

Gretna 2006

The word "Pelican" and the depiction of a pelican are
trademarks of Pelican Publishing Company, Inc., and
are registered in the U.S. Patent and Trademark Office.

Library of Congress Cataloging-in-Publication Data

Theriot, Jude W.
  The 100 greatest Cajun recipes / Jude W. Theriot.
  p. cm.
  Includes index.
  ISBN-13: 978-1-58980-305-3 (pbk. : alk. paper)
  1. Cookery, American—Louisiana style. 2. Cookery,
Cajun. I. Title: One hundred greatest Cajun recipes. II.
Title.
  TX715.2.L68T469 2006
  641.59763—dc22
                                                2005034102

Printed in Canada
Published by Pelican Publishing Company, Inc.
1000 Burmaster Street, Gretna, Louisiana 70053

To my father, Fred Lawrence Theriot Sr., Pops to all of us in the family. Dad is the only surviving child of thirteen brothers and sisters. He has had a hard life, but yet a full life filled with many blessings, hardships, good times, and not so good times. He gave to all of his children an outstanding work ethic. Dad believed that if you have a job to do, you just do it!

While I was growing up, Dad had to support a family with seven children, so he had to work hard and take every extra duty to keep all of us provided for. Dad taught us that if you wanted something, you had to work for it. He expected us to succeed and to do whatever it took to get the job done. But he also instilled in us a strong belief in God and gave us a faith that will last us a lifetime, one that we will pass on to our children.

Dad taught us that family was important, more important than money or position. He gave us a foundation in core values, a strong faith in God, and a never-dying belief that we make our own path by what we do and what we believe. It has been hard to watch my father cope with the death of my mother, his parents, and his brothers and sisters. But my father believes that death is only the door to Salvation. That message comes through so strongly as I see his faith and gain some of the strength that I know will make me a better person.

Pops, we love you, and we are so lucky to have had the opportunity to learn from such a great and caring teacher. For me, for my brothers and sisters, and for my children, my nieces, and my nephews, I thank you for all you have done for us, shared with us, and for helping us to set a strong purpose in our lives.

This book is dedicated to you!

CONTENTS

THE 100 GREATEST CAJUN RECIPES

INTRODUCTION

This is a new experience for me! It's the first time I've been given a title and asked to write the book. Usually I find the title or theme myself, then go about planning the type of recipes that will fill the pages. I have always planned a cookbook around a theme or idea. *The 100 Greatest Cajun Recipes* is the title and idea of my publisher, Milburn Calhoun. Dr. Calhoun spoke to me a number of years ago about writing this book. It sounded like a great idea, so about six years ago I wrote what I thought was the right kind of book for the 100 greatest Cajun recipes.

Well, let's just say that we had artistic differences! He owned the title and he saw it one way, and I wrote the book another. So the book sat on the shelf for six years. After I finished my last book, *Cajun Low Carb,* Dr. Calhoun again asked about my writing *The 100 Greatest Cajun Recipes.* I guess he explained it to me better this time, or maybe this time I was really listening. You know, I hate to admit that I might be wrong, but I honestly have to say Milburn was right.

So back to the drawing board I went, starting from scratch. This book needed to be written, with the style and idea that he had for the title. As I reexamined the idea, some six or seven years later, it really made sense. He wanted the core recipes that made Cajun cooking the cuisine that has turned the culinary world upside down—just the 100 greatest recipes that are the essence of Cajun cooking.

It seemed like a task that made sense and it actually seemed easy. But, alas, it was the right task but it wasn't easy at all. It took months to decide which recipes make up the essence or heart of Cajun cooking. Only 100! My first draft got it down to 242 recipes. I felt like I would never get the essence down to just 100 recipes.

Again, I have to admit that I was wrong and Milburn was right. There really was the possibility of just the top 100. What this book has, in my opinion, are the recipes that every Cajun must know to go through life. Every Cajun will easily know that the purest essence of Cajun Cuisine can be found in the following pages.

I have to admit that I have enjoyed this process, this struggle, and this excitement. I'm not going to say that this is the final word on Cajun cooking, but I do feel confident that this book contains the very heart and soul of the culinary spirit of our Cajun Culture. I hope you find your favorites, as well as recipes for dishes you may have heard about but never experienced. And I trust you will want to keep this book as a ready reference for what makes Cajun food one of the greatest cuisines the world has ever known.

THE CAJUN STORY

Whenever I go across the country, people ask me, "Just what is a Cajun?" The word Cajun is a corruption of the word Acadian. The Acadians were the people of French ancestry living in old Acadie, or Nova Scotia, Canada. They are the same people who were forcibly expelled from Canada by the British in the 1750s and 1760s. These are the people that Longfellow wrote about in his epic poem, *Evangeline*.

Of all the Louisianians of French origin, the Cajuns are just a part. Not all people living in Louisiana are Cajuns. The term is applied properly only to the descendants of those Acadians who were driven from their homeland in Canada.

That era was a terrible time for my ancestors. They had gone to Canada seeking a new and better life, free land, the ability to live as they chose, and the freedom to practice their religion. Their reasons for coming to North America were all valid and were soon realized. They etched out an existence that was comfortable and even very profitable for themselves. They were a very industrious people. They had developed a society that thrived in the heart of British territory. They were hard workers and earned all they had by the sweat of their brows. The society they formed bothered no one and they generally kept to themselves. They began to prosper in their new home.

Happenings in the American colonies didn't concern them. They were not involved. As the war between the British and France developed, they did not choose sides or get involved. Building hope and a future for their children was their goal and their priority. As the world political situation deteriorated, the Acadians were faced with a crisis.

The treaty that ended the war gave Acadie to the British, and the British demanded that the Acadians swear a loyalty oath to the king of England and to the Anglican Church. But the real goal of the British colonists was to get the land and property of the Acadians. Their hard work and industry had caused a great deal of jealousy among the British colonists.

The French crown held no special place in the Acadians' hearts or lives, but they were French people. Their religion was important to them, even more so when they were told what they would have to believe. They were Catholic and would not consider any other religion. To those proud Acadians, such a loyalty oath was not a possibility. Giving up their property and all earthly possessions was not their own choice but rather the "choice" the British government made for them. The men and boys were called to a meeting. When they arrived, they were all held hostage and told to send for their wives and daughters, who were to come with only what they could carry.

Some wives were never united with their husbands. Many children were torn from their parents and sent to foreign lands, never to see their families again. The Acadians were ripped from their homelands and shipped far and wide. The purpose was to break the spirit of the Acadians and spread them so far apart that they could never return or regain what they once had.

The tragedy was that this cruelty was mostly about jealousy and money. The British colonists wanted the prosperity of the Acadians—and the Acadians had the best land, a lot of cattle, the most aggressive and ambitious plans for the future, and the work ethic necessary to get the job done. The Acadians were doomed to the whims of a spiteful and vengeful British government.

The British Empire was not satisfied with a peaceful settlement. They took an even crueler approach in expelling the Acadians from Acadie. Families were deliberately split—husband from wife, mother from child, brother from sister! All were shipped off to various ports and destinations. All the Acadians had was what they took with them. They were allowed to take only what they could carry.

They were deposited in a land where they were looked down on and despised. Since most of them spoke only French, they were lost in these new lands where their mother tongue was not spoken. The agony that the British caused was never to be forgiven nor forgotten. It became a part of the Cajun soul. Never again would a Cajun completely trust government, politics, or the opinions of outsiders.

Acadian settlements were set up all across the Atlantic seaboard, and inland as well. Most Acadians eventually made their way to Louisiana, where the French had settled 100 years earlier. So, the

Acadians were not the first or the last French settlement in Louisiana. Some tried New Orleans and attempted to assimilate into the New Orleans Creole way of life. For the most part, that did not work; they were not the same people.

The Acadian culture had remained close to the French provincial way of life of the early 1600s. In Canada, they had adjusted their ways and adopted some ideas, but the language and lifestyle remained those of seventeenth-century France. The ways of the Creole French were as foreign to them as were those of the British in Canada and the American colonists.

Most of the Acadians then went to the bayou country of Southwest Louisiana. There they developed a very closed culture that cut them off from the rest of the known world. Their own world developed separately from the rest of the state and the country. Geography helped greatly; there was no way to travel through much of the area except by bayou or over a very few poor trails. Therefore they learned to depend on their families and on close, trusted neighbors. In addition, their experience in the past with outsiders, foreign countries, and non-Acadians had not been very rewarding, to say the least.

They trusted each other, family first, then other Acadian families second. No one else was to be trusted. They could depend only on one another. Their way of life continued and was nurtured by the extensive bayou system of Southern Louisiana. The Acadians became the Cajuns. They were now a unique people. They had suffered, yet they again found the faith to carry on. They were Acadian by heritage, but now they were truly Cajun.

No longer was their life cruel. They now had a very fertile land, an excellent climate, a very long growing season, and above all an abundance of fresh food: seafood, game, and a lot of fresh meat. Perhaps the physical conditions of the bayou country kept them from becoming well-to-do, but the bayous also provided rich culinary delights. Dishes fit for royalty were the everyday fare. Food was a commodity they all had in abundance.

In style, the cooking was steeped in French roots, but it had developed into a unique blend of fresh ingredients, pungent spices, and most of all a creativity that is the common gift of the common man. It is as unique as each man or woman who heated up the black iron skillets or pots of the bayou country. The land had created within the Cajun people a love of food and the ability to cook from the soul, not just from the pot.

As a people, we can draw from a varied background: France, Canada, Acadie, Creole New Orleans, the Spanish, the Island cooking of the Atlantic and Gulf waters, the large black population that brought to Louisiana the wonderful culinary gifts of Africa, the native Indians with their understanding of natural heritage vegetables and wonderful native spices the land had to offer, and finally from our own Bayou Country.

Cajun cooking is exciting, yet simple and basic. It is the cooking of a simple people, but a people who worked hard to bring to the table the best of the world around them. Let your palate be your guide. To cook like a Cajun is truly to live a little closer to "Heaven on Earth!"

LAGNIAPPE

With every recipe, a Lagniappe section is included. Lagniappe is a Cajun French word that means "something for nothing," or "a gift for doing business with a Cajun." In the good old days, whenever a Cajun would shop at a stand, shop, or store, the proprietor would always throw in something extra with the purchase, just for good measure. It is somewhat similar to the "baker's dozen" concept.

Today, the word is alive in our vocabulary, but the custom, alas, has mostly disappeared. However, because I give you my *lagniappe* with each recipe, you will get to experience firsthand just how it feels to receive "something for nothing." What I have done is to help you in your culinary tasks! You will find shortcuts, hints, additional ideas on similar recipes, information on which dish is appropriate for refrigeration for later use, which dish can be frozen, and how to deal with a "second-hand dish." I will also give you additional related recipes when appropriate.

These lagniappe sections are filled with hints and suggestions that will make cooking a particular recipe easier. They also contain general cooking tips and bits of enlightenment that I have gleaned over the years.

A lot of people tell me that they enjoy reading cookbooks like other people enjoy reading novels. This is a special addition that will give the reader insights that should be beneficial and helpful to his or her cooking in general. I must admit, however, that I occasionally may just use the Lagniappe section to step out of the recipe and just "talk to you."

I hope you take full advantage of this old Cajun custom and use these Lagniappe sections while using this book. They will make the overall experience of using the *The 100 Greatest Cajun Recipes* more interesting, rewarding, informative, and of course more delicious.

Bon appétit!

APPETIZERS

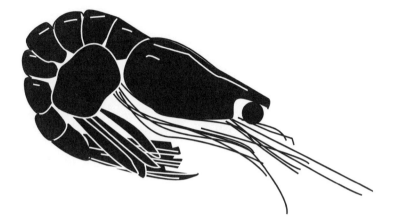

CRAWFISH BOULETTES

1 lb. crawfish tails, cleaned
6 whole green onions, finely minced
$^1/_2$ cup fresh parsley, finely minced
1 large egg, slightly beaten
$^1/_2$ cup all-purpose flour, sifted
$^1/_2$ cup shortening
1 tsp. Tabasco® Sauce
1 tsp. salt
1 tsp. black pepper, freshly ground
Flour to roll the balls in
Cooking oil for frying

Preheat the oil to 375 degrees. Mix together, in a large mixing bowl, the crawfish tails, onions, parsley, and egg until well blended. Add the flour, shortening, Tabasco® Sauce, salt, and black pepper and combine thoroughly with your hands. Form the mixture into balls, as you would make meatballs, about $^1/_2$ inch in diameter. Roll the balls in the flour and fry them in the hot cooking oil until they are crisp and nicely browned, about 5 minutes. Serve at once. Serves 6. Makes about 18 boulettes.

Lagniappe: While there are many ways to serve boulettes and to form them, I like this method best. However, some cooks like to make the boulettes into round cakes, about 3 inches wide and 1 inch high. Others like to make them elongated, about 1 inch thick and $2^1/_2$ inches long. No matter how you make your boulettes, they are delicious. The two methods are better suited for making this a main dish rather than an appetizer.

HOT CRABMEAT DIP

1 stick butter, unsalted
6 whole green onions, chopped
$^{1}/_{4}$ cup celery, chopped
$^{1}/_{4}$ cup bell pepper, chopped
2 cloves garlic, minced
2 tbsp. flour, all-purpose
$^{2}/_{3}$ cup milk
8 large mushrooms, sliced
8 ozs. cream cheese, softened
    and cut into cubes

1 tsp. Tabasco® Sauce
1 tbsp. Worcestershire sauce
$^{1}/_{2}$ tsp. black pepper
$^{1}/_{4}$ tsp. white pepper
$^{1}/_{2}$ tsp. sweet basil
$^{1}/_{2}$ tsp. onion powder
$^{1}/_{2}$ tsp. salt
1 lb. all-lump crabmeat, fresh
$^{1}/_{4}$ cup parsley, freshly minced
Crackers or small pastry shells

Melt the butter in a medium saucepan over medium heat until melted. Sauté the green onions, celery, bell pepper, and garlic for 5 minutes. Add the flour and cook, stirring constantly for 3 minutes. Remove from the heat and gently pour in the milk; stir in well, then return to the heat. Continue to stir until sauce begins to thicken. Add the mushrooms, cream cheese, Tabasco® Sauce, Worcestershire, peppers, basil, onion powder, and salt, then reduce the heat to low and stir constantly until the cream cheese has melted. Lightly fold in the crabmeat and parsley. Cook until the crabmeat is warm, about 3 minutes. Pour into a chafing dish or place the saucepan on a warmer and serve. Serve with crackers or small pastry shells. Serves 10 to 15.

Lagniappe: You can make this dip up to a day in advance and refrigerate. Be careful not to stir it too much when you reheat or you will break up the nice lumps of crabmeat. Do not freeze this dip. It breaks down the crabmeat too much and loses too much texture. You can also mix this dip with cooked fettuccine noodles to make a wonderful Crabmeat Fettuccine. Just mix about half of the dip with a package of cooked noodles and you have an instant, wonderful dinner. I also like to use this dip to make Crabmeat Crepes. I just put about 3 tablespoons of dip into the center of a cooked crepe and roll it up. I make a sauce with about 1 cup of the dip and $1/2$ cup of heavy whipping cream, with a dash of Tabasco® Sauce, which I heat over low heat until the sauce is blended. I then spoon about 2 tablespoons of the sauce over each crepe and serve. Talk about heavenly!

HOG HEAD CHEESE

4 whole pig feet, cleaned
1 whole hog head, cleaned,
  10 to 12 lbs.
Cold water to cover
2 tsp. salt
2 tsp. cayenne pepper
2 tsp. Tabasco® Sauce
2 cups green onions, chopped
1 cup fresh parsley, finely
  chopped
1/4 cup bell pepper, finely
  diced
1/4 cup red bell pepper, finely
  diced
3 tbsp. celery, minced
3 cloves garlic, finely minced
2 tsp. sage
1 package gelatin, dissolved
  in 1/2 cup cold water
1/2 cup red wine vinegar
Salt and black pepper to taste
1 12x18 glass baking dish,
  lightly greased with butter
Crackers or French bread

In a large stock pot, place the pig feet and then the hog's head. Cover the head with water, then add the 2 teaspoons salt, cayenne pepper, and Tabasco® Sauce, and bring to a hard boil. When the water comes to a hard boil, cover and let it boil for 5 minutes. Then reduce the heat to medium and let it boil for 2 more hours, covered. The meat should have started to leave the bones. Remove from the heat and cool. Reserve the stockpot liquid for later use.

When cool, remove the head and feet from the pot and pick all the meat from the bone that remains. Discard the head and feet. Put the meat into a large bowl, taking care to remove any meat that is left in the stockpot. Chop the meat well, until it is very fine. Add the green onions, parsley, red and green bell pepper, celery, and garlic. Mix well together. Blend in the sage and the dissolved gelatin. Add the vinegar, and salt and pepper to taste. Pour in about 2 cups of liquid from the stock pot that was reserved. Blend it in well with the meat mixture and pour into the greased glass baking dish.

Place in the refrigerator until the mixture has jelled, about 3 hours. When jelled, slice into 2-inch squares and serve with crackers or French bread.

Lagniappe: Yes this does take a little time, but boy is it worth it! As a kid, I couldn't wait for the holiday time of the year, because all the neighbors made their own version of hog head cheese. It was great to taste all the variations. Today, you can use a fresh picnic ham instead of the hog's head and feet, if you think that you just won't be able to use the head. Real head cheese is best, because of the great natural gelatin that comes from the fresh head and feet, but the alternative will do okay. Just add about 2 more packs of gelatin if you don't use the head and feet to prepare. This is a true Cajun appetizer that is well worth the time it takes to make.

BOUDIN

5 lbs. fresh pork shoulder
2 lbs. pork liver
Water to cover
10 whole black pepper corns
2 tsp. salt
2 large onions, chopped in
  two
5 cloves garlic, crushed
1 tsp. salt
1 tsp. cayenne pepper

1 tsp. black pepper, freshly
  ground
2 tsp. Tabasco® Sauce
1 tsp. onion powder
$^1/_2$ tsp. garlic powder
8 cups cooked white rice,
  short-grain
1 package sausage casings
1 gal. simmering hot water
1 tsp. salt

Put the pork shoulder and liver into a large stockpot and cover it with cold water. Bring the water to a boil over high heat, then reduce to a simmer. Add the black pepper corns, 2 teaspoons of salt, onions, and garlic, then cover and simmer over low heat for $3^1/_2$ to 4 hours.

Remove from the heat, and allow the pot to cool for 10 minutes, then remove the meat from the stockpot along with the onions and garlic. Reserve the liquid for later use. Debone the pork shoulder. The meat should almost fall off the bone. Grind the meat, liver, onions, and garlic together into a large mixing bowl. Season with the 1 teaspoon of salt, cayenne pepper, black pepper, Tabasco® Sauce, onion, and garlic powder; mix together well. Add the rice to the meat mixture and blend together well. If the mixture is too dry, add enough of the reserved cooking stock to moisten the mixture well.

Stuff the mixture into the sausage casings and tie a knot in the casings at intervals of about 1 foot. Put the stuffed casings into the simmering gallon of hot water to "uniform" it throughout the casings. Serve the boudin hot. If you like, you can also fry the boudin in a small amount of bacon drippings or butter until the boudin is warm throughout. Serves 10 to 12.

Lagniappe: This is true Cajun goodness. You might wonder why you make such a large batch. When you serve it, you'll understand why! Boudin and Cajuns go together so well that there is almost never enough! Serve the boudin right from the simmering pot or refrigerate it for up to 4 days. You can freeze it for later use if there happens to be any leftovers! I usually make a double batch and serve one and freeze one for later. If you do that, freeze the first batch and serve the second, so you'll be sure to have a batch to freeze. If you let everyone see how much is left, there won't be any to freeze. They'll eat it all. I like to put a couple of links into a Ziploc freezer bag, press the air out of the bag, and freeze. Be sure to mark the date on each bag so you'll eat the oldest bag in the freezer first.

To make Blood Boudin or Red Boudin mix fresh pork blood with the meat mixture and put into a large saucepan and cook, stirring often, for 5 minutes. Then mix in the cooked rice before stuffing the casings. I would caution you against doing this unless you have just butchered a whole pig and know that the blood is fresh. Blood attracts bacteria at such a rapid rate that any storing of fresh blood is too risky. If you do make blood boudin, I recommend eating it right after the casings are pulled from the simmering water bath. Blood boudin is a favorite Cajun dish. It truly does have quite a unique flavor, but you almost have to be a true Cajun to enjoy it!

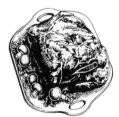

APPETIZERS

SAUSAGE CARAMEL

4 lbs. smoked pork sausage,
   sliced $1/2$ inch thick
1 stick butter, unsalted
$1^1/_2$ cups dark brown sugar,
   packed
$1^1/_2$ cups light brown sugar,
   packed

1 cup white distilled vinegar
$3/_4$ cup dry Burgundy wine
2 tsp. Tabasco® Sauce
1 med. onion, sliced

In a large skillet, fry the sausage over high heat until it is nicely browned on both sides. Remove the sausage as it is cooked and set aside for later use. Wipe most of the excess drippings from the pan with a clean paper towel and add the butter. Reduce the heat to medium and add the butter and melt. When the butter is melted, add the brown sugars and cook, stirring constantly until the sugars have melted and begin to caramelize, about 5 to 7 minutes over medium-high heat.

Remove from the heat and pour in the vinegar, but be careful, because it tends to splatter and let off a lot of steam when added. Add the wine and return to the heat. Cook until the sugar has dissolved again into the sauce. Add the Tabasco® Sauce, onion, and reserved browned sausage, reduce the heat to simmer, and cook for 20 minutes, stirring a few times. Serve hot. Serves 8.

Lagniappe: This dish will surprise you! It is an old caramel barbecue sauce that my grandmother used to make. It makes a great appetizer and when all the sausage is gone, it makes a wonderful basting barbecue sauce for chicken, pork, or sausage. This dish can stay on a warming tray all evening and the sausage will just get better. You can also make this dish completely in advance and freeze for later use. I like to freeze it in smaller batches so I can defrost in the microwave when I have surprise guests and want something quick and tasty to serve.

It also makes a great Sausage Poboy. Just put mustard and mayonnaise on a piece of French bread and scoop the sausage from the sauce onto the bread with a little of the caramel sauce and serve. You can also add a slice of tomato, a couple of slices of pickles. and lettuce leaves to really dress it up nicely. Talk about great eating!

APPETIZERS

OYSTERS EN BROCHETTE

16 strips bacon, cut in half
32 oysters, large, raw, and
   fresh
8 6-in. wooden skewers
1 large egg, well beaten
3/4 cup milk
1 tsp. Tabasco® Sauce
1 tsp. salt

1 tsp. black pepper, freshly
   ground
Flour, all-purpose, for rolling
   brochettes
Cooking oil for deep frying
16 toasted bread points
8 lemon wedges, fresh

Preheat the cooking oil to 350 degrees. Fry the bacon until it is lightly browned, but not yet crisp. Alternate 4 oysters and 4 half strips of bacon (which have been folded) on each of the 8 wooden skewers. Make a light egg batter with the egg, milk, and Tabasco® Sauce, salt and pepper and dip each of the oyster brochettes into the egg batter, and roll in the flour. Deep fry the brochettes until they are golden brown, about 5 to 7 minutes. Serve on top of 2 toast points and garnish with a lemon wedge. Serves 4.

Lagniappe: This is best eaten right from the deep-frying pot. Just make sure that the brochettes are put together before you are ready to fry. Then just before you are ready to serve, batter them and roll them in flour and fry. It really doesn't take too long to cook, but they just have to be served right from the pot. Do not batter them in advance or try to flour them before you are ready to fry. This is a light batter that will become a mess if you try to flour and hold to cook later.

OYSTERS BIENVILLE

6 strips bacon, chopped
1 stick butter, unsalted
4 cloves garlic, minced
8 large green onion bottoms, finely chopped
1 lb. large mushrooms, chopped
$^3/_4$ cup flour, all-purpose
1 qt. warm milk
$^2/_3$ cup oyster liquor
$^1/_2$ cup sherry wine
$^1/_3$ cup lemon juice, fresh
2 tsp. Tabasco® Sauce
2 cups boiled shrimp, coarsely chopped

$^1/_2$ cup fresh parsley, minced
$^1/_2$ cup green onion tops, finely minced
1 tsp. salt
$^1/_2$ tsp. white pepper
1 tsp. black pepper, freshly ground
4 doz. large oysters, fresh
4 doz. large, deep oyster shells, scrubbed clean and dried
8 metal pie tins
Rock salt to put in the bottom of each pie pan to hold the shells

Place the bacon in a large saucepan and fry over medium heat until it is crisp and brown. Add the butter. When the butter is melted, add the garlic, green onion bottoms, and mushrooms and sauté, stirring often for about 5 minutes. Add the flour and blend it in well. Reduce the heat to low and cook for 5 minutes, stirring constantly, taking care not to let the flour stick or begin to brown.

Add the warm milk a little at a time, stirring until the sauce becomes smooth. Add the oyster liquor, sherry, lemon juice and Tabasco® Sauce and blend in until the sauce again becomes smooth. You may have to use a wire whisk, as the sauce sometimes needs to be whipped to a smooth consistency. Add the shrimp, parsley, green onion tops, salt, and peppers; blend well into the sauce. Cook, stirring constantly, over low heat for about 15 minutes. The sauce should thicken nicely.

Set the oven to broil. Place each of the oysters into a cleaned oyster shell and set them in a pie pan to which you have added rock salt. Broil them for about 1½ minutes about 3 inches from the heat source. The oysters should curl up around the edges and become somewhat puffy. Remove from the oven and set the oven to 425 degrees. Using a spatula, place about 2 to 3 tablespoons of the Bienville Sauce over and around each oyster, completely covering each and filling in all the gaps between the oyster and the shell. When all the oysters are covered, bake for about 10 minutes or until the tops are lightly browned and the edges are bubbling. Serve immediately. Serves 8 as an appetizer.

Lagniappe: This is the Oysters Bienville recipe that I served at Le Champignon Restaurant and at Old Vienna Restaurant. I've had so many requests for the recipe for this sauce! It is incredible. You can do so much with this sauce in addition to making wonderful Oysters Bienville. I almost wonder if there is anything that it can't sauce well! You can make it in advance and refrigerate for up to 5 days. Just keep it in a tightly covered container.

You can also spoon the sauce over lump crabmeat and serve it in a crab shell to make Crabmeat Bienville or over shrimp in a ramekin to make Shrimp Bienville. (That's my father's favorite. I even used to serve it to him on an oyster shell. No one ever knew he was eating shrimp while they were eating oysters—until now that is!) This Bienville Sauce is also wonderful over baked chicken breasts or on top of Veal Panné. Talk about good eating!

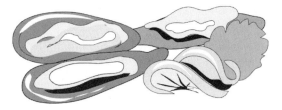

SHRIMP REMOULADE

1 cup mayonnaise
¹/₄ cup Creole mustard
1 tbsp. prepared horseradish
1 tsp. Tabasco® Sauce
1 tsp. Worcestershire sauce
3 cloves garlic, minced
2 tbsp. paprika
2 tbsp. red wine vinegar
¹/₂ tsp. onion powder
¹/₂ cup parsley, freshly chopped
1 cup green onions, chopped
¹/₄ cup celery, chopped
1 recipe Boiled Shrimp (see index)
¹/₂ head lettuce, shredded
Lemon wedges as garnish

In a large mixing bowl, combine the mayonnaise, mustard, horseradish, Tabasco® Sauce, Worcestershire sauce, garlic, paprika, vinegar, and onion powder. Whip together well with a wire whisk until well blended. Fold in the parsley, green onions, and celery until well mixed.

Peel and devein the shrimp and fold them into the Remoulade sauce. Cover tightly and refrigerate until you are ready to serve. It is best if you let the shrimp sit in the sauce for at least 2 hours to allow all the flavors to blend well. When you are ready to serve, arrange the shredded lettuce on each of four plates and spoon an equal amount of the shrimp and sauce onto each of the four plates. Garnish with a couple of lemon wedges and serve chilled. Serves 4.

Lagniappe: This is a quick and easy remoulade. It can be made in advance, without the shrimp, and refrigerated for up to a week. It is a great salad dressing even without the shrimp. You can make it with the shrimp up to 24 hours in advance. Just keep it tightly covered. When you are ready to serve, just shred the lettuce and spoon the sauce and shrimp on top. A great appetizer or a light luncheon treat.

CAJUN SHRIMP COCKTAIL

1 cup catsup
$^{1}/_{2}$ cup chili sauce
$^{1}/_{4}$ cup horseradish sauce
2 tsp. Tabasco® Sauce
$^{1}/_{2}$ cup celery, minced
1 clove garlic, minced
2 whole green onions, minced
2 tbsp. fresh parsley, minced
1 tsp. salt
1 tsp. black pepper, finely
  ground

1 tbsp. Worcestershire sauce
$^{1}/_{2}$ tsp. sweet basil
1 whole bay leaf, finely
  crushed
2 tbsp. lemon juice, freshly
  squeezed
1 recipe Boiled Shrimp (see
  index)
$^{1}/_{2}$ head lettuce, shredded
Lemon wedges as garnish

In a medium mixing bowl, mix all the ingredients except the shrimp, lettuce, and lemon wedges until well mixed. Let stand for 3 hours, tightly covered in the refrigerator. Peel and devein the shrimp. Place them into the cocktail sauce and mix well. Tightly cover again and let the shrimp cocktail mixture refrigerate for another hour. When ready to serve, equally spread the shredded lettuce onto four plates and spoon an equal amount of shrimp and sauce on top of each plate. Garnish with the lemon wedge. Serve chilled. Serves 4.

Lagniappe: You can make this sauce for up to a week in advance and keep tightly covered in the refrigerator. Do not add the shrimp until about an hour before you are ready to serve. You can also use this same sauce to make Cajun Crab Cocktail by using lump crabmeat instead of the shrimp, or you can make a wonderful Cajun Oyster Cocktail by using freshly shucked oysters in place of the shrimp. For those who don't like raw oysters, you can

32

parboil the oysters in lightly salted water over low heat before placing the oysters in the sauce. Just cook the oysters in the lightly salted water with their own juice for about 1 minute. They should puff up and begin to curl on the edges. What a treat!

CAJUN PATE

Salt pork, cut into thin slices
   to line the paté pan
6 slices bacon, diced
1 large onion, chopped
$^1/_2$ cup bell pepper, chopped
$^1/_4$ cup celery, chopped
3 cloves garlic, chopped
1 lb. calves' liver
1 lb. chicken liver
1 tsp. salt
1 tsp. black pepper, finely
   ground

1 tsp. Tabasco® Sauce
3 large eggs, yolk only
2 large eggs
$^1/_2$ cup Madeira wine
$^1/_2$ tsp. salt
$^1/_2$ tsp. chervil
$^1/_2$ tsp. tarragon
$^1/_2$ tsp. sweet basil
$^1/_2$ tsp. nutmeg
$^1/_4$ tsp. allspice
French bread slices and sweet
   gherkin pickles

Preheat the oven to 375 degrees. Rinse the salt pork slices in cold water to remove as much of the salt as possible. Drain thoroughly and pat dry with paper towels. Line a paté pan with the pork slices. Cook the chopped bacon in a large, heavy skillet over medium-high heat until the bacon is crisp. Sauté the onion, bell pepper, celery, and garlic in the bacon grease until the onions are tender, about 5 minutes. Cut the calves' liver into 1-inch pieces and halve the chicken livers.

Add the livers to the sauté pan, season with the salt, black pepper, and Tabasco® Sauce, and cook until all the pink disappears from the livers, about 7 minutes, stirring constantly. Place the liver-onion mixture into a food processor or blender and purée. Add the egg yolks and eggs a little at a time until they are well blended. Add the Madeira wine and blend in well.

Add the remaining ingredients except for the French bread slices and pickles; blend in thoroughly. Pour the liver mixture into the paté pan and cover with aluminum foil. Place the mold into a larger baking dish. Add water halfway to the top of the mold and bake in the preheated 375-degree oven for 2 hours. Remove from the pan and cool the paté for at least 8 hours. Invert the paté onto a platter and serve, chilled, with warm French bread and sweet gherkin pickles. Serves 8 to 12.

Lagniappe: This is an outstanding paté. You'll wonder why you pay all that money to get a prepared paté. Now let's be serious, here. Do not keep this for too long. Liver has to be watched carefully. Do not refrigerate for more than 4 days. Be sure to keep it well chilled. While the taste is wonderful, paté does have a tendency to spoil easily. So take care in handling this dish. It's great as an appetizer, and it makes delicious sandwiches as well.

STOCKS, GUMBOS, SOUPS, SALADS, AND SALAD DRESSINGS

CHICKEN STOCK

6 lbs. chicken thighs, legs, and backs
1 gal. water
2 med. onions, quartered
3 med. carrots, cut into thirds
3 stalks celery, chopped into thirds
3 whole green onions, washed, roots removed
1/2 bunch parsley, with stems on, washed
3 cloves garlic, crushed
3 bay leaves
3 stems fresh basil
2 sprigs fresh thyme
15 whole black peppercorns
1 tsp. salt
2 whole cloves
1 tsp. Tabasco® Sauce

Preheat the oven to 500 degrees. Wash the chicken well in cold water. Remove as much skin as possible and place the chicken in a 500-degree oven on a shallow baking pan. Let the chicken brown nicely, turning after 10 minutes, then continue to brown the other side for another 10 minutes. When done, remove from the oven and set aside. Add the remaining ingredients into a large stock pot or gumbo pot and bring to a hard boil, then reduce to a low simmer and add the chicken pieces to the pot. Simmer for 6 hours, stirring a few times.

When done, remove the pot from the heat and let cool. When cool enough, strain with a fine sieve strainer. Then cover the stock and refrigerate overnight. The next day, remove any fat that has floated to the top of the stock pot. This should make about 2 quarts of excellent stock.

Lagniappe: This may be eaten as a soup or used as a base for other soups and sauces. Homemade stock is hard to beat. The making of stock is not really that hard. It just takes a little time. Make it on a day that you are doing something else away from the kitchen. Then you can either refrigerate the stock or use it for up to 5 days later. It freezes well. I like to freeze it in ice cube trays, putting $1/4$ cup of stock in each cube. I freeze it in freezer-ready Ziploc bags and have stock for use when I need it. Just thaw in the refrigerator and use as you would any broth or stock. This will add greatly to any soup or sauce you need to make. If you do decide to serve this as a soup by itself, take the meat from the strainer, and remove it from the bone and put it into the stock. You can use the meat for any cooked chicken dish that you like, if you don't plan on serving it in the stock.

BEEF STOCK

5 lbs. beef soup meat
3 lbs. beef long ribs
1 gal. water
2 large onions, chopped
3 stalks celery, broken
4 carrots, broken
2 cloves garlic, crushed
3 whole bay leaves
2 tsp. whole black peppercorns

$1/4$ bunch fresh parsley, with
   stems on
$1/2$ cup green onion tops,
   chopped
$1/2$ med. turnip, chopped
2 tbsp. cabbage, chopped
1 tsp. salt
3 stems fresh basil
2 sprigs fresh thyme
1 tsp. Tabasco® Sauce

Preheat the oven to 500 degrees. Chop the soup meat into small pieces and set aside. Place the beef ribs in a shallow baking pan and bake them at 500 degrees until they are quite brown, but not burnt, about 20 minutes. Turn the ribs after they have been in the oven 12 minutes.

While the ribs are browning, sauté the soup meat over medium high heat in a large stock pot or gumbo pot until the meat is nicely browned. Do not let the meat stick to the pot. When browned, add the water and bring to a hard boil. When the liquid is boiling, add the rest of the ingredients except for the ribs and reduce the heat to a low simmer. Add the browned ribs to the stock pot when they are finished browning. Simmer the stock for 5 to 6 hours. If the water level starts to drop, add a little more water and lower the heat a little more.

When the time is up, remove from the heat and let the stock cool so you can handle it. Strain the cooled broth from the meat and vegetables with a fine wire sieve and put the broth in the refrigerator to chill. The fat should rise to the top and harden. Remove as much of the fat as possible.

This should make about 2 quarts of stock. It may be eaten as is but more often is used as the base for other soups or sauces.

Lagniappe: You can make this stock well ahead of the time you need it. It can be refrigerated for up to 5 days or it can be frozen for later use. Let the stock thaw in the refrigerator and use as you would use any broth or stock. I like to freeze the stock in ice cube trays. When they are frozen, I put them into freezer lock Ziploc bags for use as needed. I try to keep $1/4$ cup per cube so I can get the amount I need when it calls for homemade stock. This is an all-day project, but you should be able to make enough to last you for quite a while. There is no substitute for homemade stock. We use purchased broth or stock and it might be acceptable, but it is not in the same league as homemade.

Don't throw away the leftover meat from the broth pot. Even though the bulk of the flavor is gone, the meat can be finely chopped and used to make sandwiches or to add meat flavor to a variety of dishes.

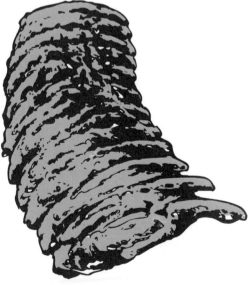

SEAFOOD STOCK

Shells from 2 lbs. shrimp
10 crab claws, cleaned (or 2 lobster shells if available)
1½ gal. water
2 stalks celery
2 med. carrots, cut into 4 pieces each
1 med. white onion, peeled and cut into fourths
3 cloves garlic, unpeeled but crushed
2 bay leaves
¼ bunch fresh parsley
4 whole green onions, washed and trimmed
1 tbsp. fresh turnip, minced
10 whole black peppercorns
1 sprig fresh sweet basil
1 sprig fresh thyme
2 whole cloves
¼ tsp. mustard seeds

Place all the ingredients into a large stockpot. Bring to a boil over high heat, then reduce the heat to a simmer. Let the stock simmer for at least 4 hours, adding a cup of water at a time as the water begins to evaporate. Remove from the heat and let it cool for at least 30 minutes. Then strain through a colander to remove the large pieces. Then strain again through cheese cloth to remove the small pieces. Refrigerate for at least 1 hour. Makes about 3 cups of stock. This stock is used to enhance seafood dishes and is not really good enough to eat alone.

Lagniappe: This stock can be made well in advance and frozen for later use. I like to freeze it in ice cubes that take about 4 to make cup of liquid. I freeze them in an ice cube tray and then put them into Ziploc freezer bags to use as needed. It helps to make the stock when you have shrimp peelings and crab claws available. If I don't have both available at the same time, then I freeze the part I have and save until I have both. If you need to use all the stock you make in the recipe you are making, then the stock can be refrigerated for up to 4 days. It really intensifies as it sits in the refrigerator, so you are really improving the quality by refrigerating. It is really worth the extra effort to make your own stock. It will add so much flavor to your dish and let the people you are cooking for know that you care!

CHICKEN AND OKRA GUMBO

1 cup cooking oil
1 cup flour, all-purpose
2 large yellow onions, chopped
1 large bell pepper, chopped
3 stalks celery, minced
4 cloves garlic, minced
1 large stewing hen (6$^{1}/_{2}$ to 7 lbs.), cut into serving pieces
3 tsp. Cajun Seasoning Mix (see index)
3 qts. Chicken Stock (see index)
1 lb. tasso (smoked spicy pork or beef)
1 whole bay leaf
$^{1}/_{2}$ tsp. sweet basil
1 tsp. garlic powder
1 tsp. onion powder
$^{1}/_{2}$ tsp. white pepper
1 tsp. cayenne pepper
$^{1}/_{2}$ tsp. black pepper
1 tsp. salt
2 tsp. Tabasco® Sauce
3 cups Smothered Okra (see index)
1 tsp. filé powder
1 cup green onions, chopped
$^{1}/_{2}$ cup fresh parsley, minced
Filé powder to taste
Cooked White Rice (see index)

In a gumbo pot or large stockpot (2$^{1}/_{2}$ to 3 gallons), heat the cooking oil over high heat until the oil starts to smoke. Add the flour and stir constantly with a wire whisk, making sure the roux is constantly moving and not sticking to any part of the pot. (I find that tilting the pot from one side to another helps you see if there is any sticking.) Continue to cook over high heat until the roux becomes a dark reddish brown, about 3 to 5 minutes. When the proper color is reached, add the onions, bell pepper, celery, and garlic. Sauté over medium-high heat in the roux for about 3 minutes, stirring constantly with a large wooden spoon.

Season the chicken evenly with the Cajun Seasoning Mix taking care to evenly spread the seasoning over all the pieces. Fry one-third of the chicken in the roux mixture over medium heat for 5 minutes, then remove the chicken to a large bowl and reserve for later use. Fry another third for 5 minutes, remove to the bowl and reserve, and then fry the last third for 5 minutes. Put all the chicken back into the pot and add the chicken stock. Stir until the roux is absorbed into the stock.

Add the tasso, bay leaf, basil, garlic powder, onion powder, white pepper, cayenne, black pepper, salt and Tabasco® Sauce. Heat over medium-high heat until the gumbo comes to a boil, then reduce it to a low simmer. Simmer for 2 hours, then add the smothered okra and 1 teaspoon of filé powder, and stir, and cook for another $2^1/_2$ hours.

Add the green onions and parsley and stir in well. Cook for 12 more minutes on a very low simmer. Serve hot in individual serving bowls with filé powder over the cooked white rice. Serves 10.

Lagniappe: This is Cajun gumbo at its best! Gumbo is one of the mainstays of the Cajun people. It can and should be made the day before you serve it and put into the refrigerator. Storing it for a day actually improves the flavor and helps intensify it. The gumbo will keep in the refrigerator for up to 5 days. It also freezes well. To serve after freezing, just store in the refrigerator until it is thawed and put on low heat until it becomes heated throughout.

You can use this exact recipe to make Chicken and Andouille Gumbo. Just follow the recipe above except substitute 2 pounds of andouille sausage for the tasso. Andouille is a very spicy Cajun sausage that really lends itself well to gumbo. Its spicy and smoky flavor is made for gumbo.

SEAFOOD GUMBO

1 cup cooking oil
1 1/2 cups flour, all-purpose
2 large onions, chopped
1 large bell pepper, chopped
1 cup celery, minced
5 cloves garlic, minced
2 tsp. Cajun Seasoning Mix
  (see index)
1 tsp. cayenne pepper
1 tsp. Tabasco® Sauce
2 whole bay leaves
1/4 tsp. thyme
3 qts. Seafood Stock (see
  index)

1 doz. crabs, cleaned
2 1/2 lbs. shrimp (21-25's),
  peeled and deveined
1 pt. oysters and their liquid
1 1/2 cups green onions,
  minced
1/2 cup fresh parsley, minced
1 lb. all-lump crabmeat
Cajun Seasoning Mix to
  adjust seasoning to taste
Cooked White Rice (see index)
Filé powder to taste

In a large gumbo pot or large stock pot (2 1/2 to 3 gallons), heat the cooking oil until it starts to smoke, then add the flour. Cook, stirring constantly with a wire whisk, over medium-high heat until the flour turns to a dark reddish brown. Be sure to stir constantly and not let the roux stick. When the correct color is achieved, add the onions, bell pepper, celery, and garlic; continue to cook, stirring constantly until the vegetables have wilted nicely, about 5 minutes.

Add the Cajun Seasoning Mix, cayenne pepper, Tabasco® Sauce, bay leaves, thyme, and Seafood Stock and stir until the roux has been well blended and absorbed into the stock. When the roux has blended, add the crabs, stir in well, and cook for 1 1/2 hours over medium heat, stirring often. Add the shrimp, oysters, and their liquid and cook for 12 minutes, stirring often. Add the green onions, parsley, and lump crabmeat and mix carefully, taking care not to break apart the lump crabmeat.

Adjust the seasonings to taste using the Cajun Seasoning Mix and reduce the heat to simmer and let the gumbo simmer for 5 more minutes. Serve hot over cooked white rice. Add filé powder to taste. Serves 8 to 10.

Lagniappe: A seafood lovers dream. Cajun Seafood Gumbo is the famous soup that makes Louisiana famous. The intense flavor and delicate seafood makes this a treat for all. You can make in advance and refrigerate for later use. It can also be frozen. If I plan on refrigerating or freezing, I don't add the lump crabmeat until right before I plan on serving. Lump crabmeat starts to break apart with heating and freezing further tears it apart. You get all the flavor, but you don't get to bite into those wonderful large bites of crabmeat. Some people like to add the taste of smoked sausage or andouille or even tasso to their seafood gumbo. I happen to like only the taste of seafood in mine, but if you like, just add it in with the whole cleaned crabs. It will add a nice spicy and smoky flavor to the gumbo. However you like it, it will get raves!

SHRIMP GUMBO

1 cup cooking oil
1¼ cups flour, all-purpose
2 large onions, chopped
3 stalks celery, minced
4 cloves garlic, crushed, then minced
1 med. bell pepper, chopped
1 can (15 oz.) stewed tomatoes
1 gal. seafood stock, warmed, or chicken broth
2 tsp. salt
1 tsp. garlic powder
1 tsp. onion powder
1 tsp. black pepper
1 tsp. cayenne pepper
1 tsp. Tabasco® Sauce
2 whole bay leaves
½ tsp. sweet basil leaves
1 tbsp. Worcestershire sauce
4½ lbs. shrimp, peeled and deveined (31-36's)
1 cup green onions, chopped fine
½ cup fresh parsley, minced
Salt and pepper to taste
Cooked White Rice (see index)
Filé powder to taste

In a very heavy gumbo pot or large, heavy stockpot, heat the oil over medium-high heat for 4 minutes, then add the flour. Cook the flour, stirring constantly until the roux turns dark reddish brown. When the desired color is reached, add the onions, celery, garlic, and bell pepper and sauté the vegetables for 5 more minutes, stirring constantly. Add the stewed tomatoes and sauté for 5 more minutes, taking care to break up the tomatoes as much as possible while constantly stirring. Slowly add the warm seafood stock, stirring very often until all the roux has dissolved into the liquid.

Add the seasoning ingredients through the Worcestershire sauce and stir in well. Bring the mixture to a boil, then immediately reduce the heat to a rolling simmer, add ½ pound of the shrimp, and cook the mixture, stirring occasionally, for 1 hour. Add the rest of the shrimp tails, then reduce the heat to a very low simmer and cook for 25 more minutes. Add the green onions and parsley and cook for 2 more minutes. Check the gumbo for seasoning by taste, using the salt and pepper. Serve hot in individual serving bowls over cooked white rice as desired. Season with filé powder and serve. Serves 8 to 10.

Lagniappe: This is an excellent dish to make in advance and refrigerate or freeze for later use. It actually improves the dish to make it at least 24 hours in advance. The flavors tend to intensify and blend better. To serve after refrigeration, just reheat over low heat until hot enough to eat. Sometimes people try to skip putting the $1/2$ pound of shrimp into the pot for the hour of cooking time because they almost disappear and you might feel like they are wasted. But the flavor they impart to the dish clearly makes this a vital step. Skip this step and you'll go from great gumbo to good gumbo. My money is always on "good to great!"

If you really want to have even more variety, you can use $2^1/2$ pounds of shrimp (31-36's) and 2 pounds of 21-25's. (You read that as 31 to 36 shrimp tails per pound. It's the standard way of sizing shrimp.) To make Crawfish Gumbo, just substitute 5 pounds of crawfish for the $4^1/2$ lbs. of shrimp and proceed as above, except put a whole pound of crawfish instead the $1/2$ pound of shrimp. You might ask why a whole pound? It's really very simple. Crawfish comes in 1-pound packages, so using only $1/2$ pound and trying to save the rest doesn't make sense.

DUCK GUMBO

1 cup cooking oil
1 cup flour, all-purpose
2 large yellow onions, chopped
1 med. bell pepper, chopped
1½ cups celery, minced
4 cloves garlic, minced
2 tsp. salt
1 tsp. black pepper, freshly ground
1 tsp. cayenne pepper
½ tsp. white pepper
1 tsp. Tabasco® Sauce
1 tsp. garlic powder
1 tsp. onion powder
½ tsp. sweet basil
2 whole bay leaves
4 med. wild ducks, cleaned and cut into fourths
2 lbs. pure pork smoked rope sausage, sliced 1 inch long
3½ qts. chicken stock, chicken broth, or hot water
8 large eggs, hard boiled, peeled
1 cup green onions, chopped
½ cup fresh parsley, minced
Filé powder to taste
Cooked White Rice (see index)

In a heavy gumbo pot or heavy stock pot, heat the cooking oil over medium-high heat until it is hot, then add the flour, stirring constantly. Cook until the roux turns a very dark, dark brown, but take care not to burn. Just keep the flour moving constantly in the pot, using a wire whisk. Add the onions, bell pepper, celery, and garlic and sauté until the vegetables are soft and the onions clear, about 8 to 10 minutes. Add the seasonings, from salt to bay leaves, and the duck quarters.

Cook, stirring often, over medium heat for 12 to 15 minutes. Add the sausage and continue to cook for 5 more minutes. Add the stock and stir until the roux has dissolved. Bring the gumbo to a boil, then reduce the heat to a low simmer. Add the hard-boiled peeled eggs and cook at low simmer for 2 hours, stirring a few times every hour. The meat should be tender. Add the green onions and parsley and cook for 5 more minutes. Skim off any excess fat that may have risen to the top of the gumbo with a large metal spoon. Serve hot over cooked white rice, in individual serving bowls. Season to taste with filé powder. Serves 8 to 10.

Lagniappe: The wild taste of the ducks and the pork sausage come together to make this a unique-tasting gumbo. The slow cooking makes the meat tender, and the spicy nature of gumbo helps to remove the "wild" taste from the ducks and transfer and transform that wild taste to a unique flavor that is only found in wild duck gumbo. Filé powder is dried, ground-up sassafras leaves. It gives gumbo its special flavor, but it is an acquired taste. Try it a little at a time, until you enjoy the dramatic flavor it adds to gumbo. It is a Louisiana spice the Cajuns got from the local Indians. While it resembles the bay leaf, it is also a totally unique flavor sensation. You can now find filé powder throughout the country in most spice sections. It is an example of just how much the Cajun culture in food has traveled.

SHRIMP BISQUE

1 stick butter, lightly salted
2 tsp. Cajun Seasoning Mix
  (see index)
2 lbs. shrimp (21-25's),
  peeled and deveined
1 large onion, minced
1 cup celery, minced
1 large red bell pepper, finely
  diced
4 cloves garlic, minced
$^2/_3$ cup flour, all-purpose
1 tsp. paprika
1 tbsp. tomato paste
1 qt. Seafood Stock (see
  index), hot

2 whole bay leaves
$^1/_2$ tsp. sweet basil
$^1/_4$ tsp. thyme
$^1/_2$ tsp. cayenne pepper
1 tsp. Tabasco® Sauce
2 cloves
4 whole black peppercorns
$^1/_2$ tsp. Cajun Seasoning Mix
  (see index)
$^1/_2$ cup sherry wine
2 tbsp. brandy
1 cup heavy whipping cream

In a large, heavy sauce pan, over medium heat, add the butter and heat until it is hot. Use the 2 teaspoons of Cajun Seasoning Mix to season the shrimp, and then add them to the sauce pan, along with the onions and celery. Sauté for 5 minutes, then add the bell pepper and garlic and sauté for 3 more minutes. Add the flour and cook, stirring constantly for 4 minutes, making sure to see that all the flour is absorbed into the butter. Add the paprika and tomato paste and blend in well.

Slowly add the hot seafood stock; stir until all the roux has been dissolved and the bisque is smooth. Add the bay leaves, basil, thyme, cayenne, Tabasco® Sauce, cloves, and peppercorns. Adjust the seasoning with up to $^1/_2$ teaspoon of Cajun Seasoning Mix, to taste. Cook over low simmering heat for $1^1/_2$ hours, partially covered, stirring often. Add the sherry, brandy, and heavy cream and blend in well. It may slightly curdle when you add the sherry, but just stir until the curdling goes away. Serve at once. Serves 6 to 8.

Lagniappe: This is wonderful at brunch or for a soup served before a nice meal. The taste of this dish is quite exceptional. While this dish is not difficult, it does take time and care to make. It can be made in advance and stored in the refrigerator for up to 2 days before serving. The flavors tend to intensify in the refrigerator. I do not recommend freezing. While you can freeze, it really destroys the texture and reduces the quality of the bisque.

You can use this recipe to make Crab Bisque by using 2 pounds of jumbo all-lump crabmeat. Just make the recipe as above, leaving the shrimp out. Do not add the lump crabmeat until the end of the recipe at the time you add the heavy cream. Just cook for 5 minutes after adding the crabmeat over low heat.

CRAWFISH BISQUE

For the stuffed crawfish heads:

48 large, live crawfish or cleaned crawfish heads from the market
Water to cover the crawfish
2 lbs. crawfish tails, fresh peeled, with their fat
2 large yellow onions, finely chopped
1 large bell pepper, finely chopped
1 cup celery, minced
1^1/$_2$ tbsp. garlic, minced
1 stick butter, unsalted
2^1/$_2$ cups French bread, cut into small dices
1 cup milk
2 tsp. Cajun Seasoning Mix (see index)
1 tsp. Tabasco® Sauce
1 tbsp. Worcestershire sauce
1 tsp. black pepper
^{1}/$_2$ cup fresh parsley, minced
1 cup green onion tops, minced
^{1}/$_2$ cup evaporated milk
1 large egg
1 large egg, yolk only
Flour for rolling

For the bisque:

1 cup peanut oil
^{3}/$_4$ cup flour, all-purpose
2 med. onions, chopped fine
1 med. red bell pepper, finely diced
^{2}/$_3$ cup celery, minced
3 cloves garlic, minced
1 can (15 oz.) stewed tomatoes
3 tbsp. tomato paste
2 lbs. crawfish tails
^{1}/$_2$ gal. Seafood Stock (see index) or chicken broth
1^1/$_2$ tsp. Cajun Seasoning Mix (see index)
^{1}/$_2$ tsp. salt
1 tsp. Tabasco® Sauce
2 whole bay leaves
1 tsp. sweet basil
^{1}/$_4$ tsp. thyme
^{2}/$_3$ cup green onions, minced
^{1}/$_3$ cup fresh parsley, finely minced
^{1}/$_4$ cup brandy
1^1/$_2$ cups heavy whipping cream
Cooked White Rice (see index)

To make the stuffed crawfish heads:

Soak the live crawfish in fresh water for 15 minutes, then clean each one well. Put them in a large stockpot and cover with plenty of fresh cold water (at least one gallon). Place pot over medium heat and bring the water to a boil, then reduce the heat to simmer and let the crawfish cook for 1 to 3 hours at a low simmer.

Remove the crawfish from the water after cooking. Let the crawfish cool until you can handle them easily. Clean one crawfish at a time as follows: break off and discard the tail; separate the head from the body, just behind the eyes; use your thumb to clean out the body. This body shell is what you will stuff with the stuffing and what will be called stuffed heads (even though it is the body of the crawfish). Repeat the process until all the crawfish are cleaned. Wash the shells (heads) and set the aside for later use. As an alternative method, just buy about 3 lbs. of boiled crawfish still in the shell and follow the method for cleaning the body for stuffing. During Crawfish season, this is the way to get your crawfish body (heads) for stuffing.

To make the stuffing:

Grind together the crawfish tails and fat, the chopped onions, bell pepper, celery, and garlic until well ground. (You can use a food processor to chop everything very fine, if a grinder is not available. Just be careful not to over chop and liquify. Use the pulse feature until you get a fine mixture.) Preheat the oven to 350 degrees. In a heavy metal sauce pot over medium heat, sauté the ground mixture in butter for 12 minutes, stirring often. While sautéing the vegetables and crawfish meat, soak the French bread in the cup of milk until it is softened. Then squeeze as much of the milk out of the bread as you can with your hands and set aside for later use.

When the sautéing time is up, add the soaked bread, Cajun Seasoning Mix, Tabasco® Sauce, Worcestershire sauce, black pepper, parsley, green onions, evaporated milk, and egg. Remove from the heat and stir the stuffing until it is well blended. Stuff the heads (body) with about 1½ tablespoons of stuffing into each shell. Roll the shells in the flour and place on a baking pan and bake at 350 degrees for 20 minutes or until golden brown. Remove from the heat and let the heads cool. Reserve to add to the bisque.

To make the bisque:

As the shells go into the oven, begin to make the soup. In a large, heavy saucepot over medium-high heat, heat the peanut oil until hot. Add the flour to make a roux, stirring constantly until the roux is a golden brown (not a dark or reddish brown). Add the onions, bell pepper, celery, and garlic and sauté for 5 minutes, stirring constantly. Add the tomatoes without the liquid (reserve the liquid for later use) and sauté for 10 minutes, stirring constantly. Add the tomato liquid, tomato paste, and crawfish tails and Seafood Stock.

Bring to a slow boil, then reduce the heat to low and add the Seafood Seasoning Mix, salt, Tabasco® Sauce, bay leaves, sweet basil, and thyme. Simmer for 1 hour over very low heat. Stir often. Add the stuffed heads, green onion, parsley, brandy, and heavy whipping cream and simmer for 10 more minutes, stirring often. Serve hot over cooked white rice. Serves 8 to 10.

Lagniappe: This is real Cajun eating. While this is not a dish you'd serve everyday, because it does take planning and time, it is genuine Cajun cooking at its best. This is the kind of dish that you know lots of love and hard work went into to create a divine dish. It should be made in advance and refrigerated for later use. You can freeze, but do not add the green onions, parsley, brandy, and whipping cream. Add that just before serving.

When you are ready to serve, heat the bisque over low heat for 12 to 15 minutes. Add the green onions, parsley, brandy, and heavy cream and heat for 5 minutes, then serve. You can also make parts of this dish at a time and assemble the whole dish when you are ready to serve. I usually like to make the stuffed heads after a crawfish boil, when there are plenty of crawfish shells to choose from. I like to pick the nice big shells for stuffing. Remember this is a company or Sunday dinner meal. It really wows your guests and lets your family know how much you love them. *Bon appétit!*

STOCKS. GUMBOS. SOUPS. SALADS

HOMEMADE VEGETABLE SOUP

3 lbs. round steak, cut into
  1½-inch pieces
2 tsp. Cajun Seasoning Mix
  (see index)
⅔ cup flour
½ cup butter
1 large onion, chopped
1 large bell pepper, chopped
2 cups celery, sliced
3 cloves garlic, minced
1 cup tomato paste
1 cup diced tomatoes
1 head cabbage, shredded
8 ears fresh corn
1 lb. carrots, cut in 2-inch
  pieces
1 lb. small new potatoes,
  washed and cleaned

4 med. turnips, chopped into
  1-inch pieces
1 gal. Beef Stock (see index)
2 tsp. Cajun Seasoning Mix
  (see index)
¼ tsp. cayenne pepper
1 tsp. Tabasco® Sauce
2 whole bay leaves
½ tsp. sweet basil
1 cup uncooked elbow
  macaroni
2 med. yellow squash, cut
  into 1-inch circles
1 med. zucchini squash, cut
  into ½-inch-thick circles

In a large mixing bowl, season the pieces of round steak with the Cajun Seasoning Mix and sprinkle the flour over the meat to coat well. In a large stock pot or gumbo pot (3-gallon size), add the butter and melt it over medium high heat. When the butter is hot, sauté the round steak until it has nicely browned. Remove the pieces of meat to another large bowl until all the meat has been browned. Reserve the meat for later use. Add the onions, bell pepper, celery, and garlic and sauté for 5 minutes. If you need to, add a little more butter to be able to sauté the vegetables.

When the vegetables are sautéed, add the tomato paste, diced tomatoes, and cabbage. Cook, stirring often, for 5 more minutes. While the cabbage is cooking, cut the corn off the cobs by holding the corn at one end and using a sharp knife. Cut down half way from the top, then turn the cob over and do the same to the other side. Be sure to scrape all the way to the cob.

Add the cut corn to the cabbage and tomato sauce and continue to stir. Add browned meat and the remaining ingredients except for the yellow and zucchini squash and stir well together. Bring to a hard boil, then reduce the heat to simmer and cover. Cook for 1 hour, stirring a few times to make sure everything is well blended. Add the squash and stir in well. Cook for 30 more minutes. Serve hot. Serves 10 to 12.

Lagniappe: This is a wonderful lunch or dinner soup. It is so full of flavor and loaded with nice vegetables. This is a great winter dish for those cold nights when you need something to warm you up and make you feel cared for. You can make this soup in advance and refrigerate or freeze for later use. Just thaw in the refrigerator and warm up over a low heat, covered until the soup is warm. There's nothing that brings people into the kitchen like a large pot of simmering soup.

COLESLAW

1 large head cabbage,
    shredded
3 whole green onions,
    minced
$^2/_3$ cup mayonnaise
$^1/_2$ cup sour cream
2 tbsp. sugar
2 tbsp. lemon juice, freshly
    squeezed

2 tbsp. pickle juice
1 tsp. Tabasco® Sauce
1 tsp. salt
$^1/_2$ tsp. black pepper
$^1/_2$ tsp. cayenne pepper

Mix together the cabbage and green onions in a large mixing bowl. In a small mixing bowl, whip together the remaining ingredients with a wire whisk until smooth. Pour over the cabbage and mix together well until completely blended. Chill for 20 minutes, then serve. Serves 6.

Lagniappe: This coleslaw is quick and easy to make, but the taste will knock you over. The blending of the ingredients makes for a super-tasting slaw. You can make and store for up to 4 days in the refrigerator. It's a nice quick snack or great with sandwiches. I mainly like to use dill pickle juice, but you can use the pickle juice that you like best.

STOCKS. GUMBOS. SOUPS. SALADS

POTATO SALAD

2¹/₂ lbs. red potatoes
5 large eggs
Cold water to boil potatoes
2 tsp. salt
10 whole black peppercorns
¹/₂ cup onions, finely chopped
¹/₂ cup sweet pickle relish
¹/₂ cup celery, finely chopped
2 tbsp. pimento, diced
1 tbsp. prepared yellow
   mustard

¹/₂ tsp. black pepper, freshly
   ground
1 tsp. salt
¹/₄ tsp. white pepper
¹/₂ tsp. Tabasco® Sauce
2 tbsp. parsley, minced
¹/₄ cup green onion tops,
   minced
1¹/₄ cups mayonnaise

Wash the potatoes and put them in a large pot. Add the eggs in their shells and fill the pot with cold water to just above the potatoes and eggs. Add the 2 teaspoons salt and the black peppercorns and place over high heat; bring to a hard boil, then reduce to a low rolling boil. Boil until the potatoes are tender when pierced with a table fork. Remove the potatoes and eggs from the water and let them cool until they are cool enough to handle.

Use a knife and peel the potatoes, taking care to remove just the thin skin, then chop them into large dices and put them into a large mixing bowl. Peel the eggs and chop them well; add them to the bowl with the potatoes. Add all the remaining ingredients except for the mayonnaise and toss lightly together until well mixed. Add the mayonnaise and mix well. Serve at once or refrigerate. Serve chilled. Serves 8.

Lagniappe: You can make this salad up to two days in

advance and refrigerate. Of course, it is best right after it is made, but it does refrigerate well. Never freeze. Be careful not to leave the salad unrefrigerated for too long or it will spoil. I like potato salad best just after it is made, when it is still slightly warm. This salad is excellent with many dishes and it is especially great with gumbo. Cajuns will often serve the salad in their gumbo bowl. You might think that strange, but try it once and you'll be surprised. I honestly believe this custom began because of the lack of serving plates in most Cajun kitchens. Like many customs in food, convenience becomes the mother of traditions.

SHRIMP SALAD

2 lbs. Boiled Shrimp (see index), peeled and chopped
4 large eggs, boiled and chopped
$1/2$ cup purple onions, chopped
$1/2$ cup celery, minced
$1/2$ cup green onions, minced
1 clove garlic, finely minced
$1/2$ cup sweet pickle relish
1 tsp. Cajun Seasoning Mix (see index)
1 cup mayonnaise
1 tbsp. Creole mustard

In a large mixing bowl, blend all the ingredients except for the shredded lettuce leaves, together, mixing well. Put into a smaller container with a tight cover and refrigerate for at least 4 hours, then serve chilled. Serve over shredded lettuce. Serves 6.

Lagniappe: This is a nice salad before meals or a meal in itself. You can make it up to 2 days in advance and refrigerate until you are ready to serve. You can use the same recipe and substitute 2 pounds of crawfish tails that you have chopped to make Crawfish Salad. Either way you are in for a treat!

SHRIMP MOLD

1 can (10³/4 oz.) tomato soup, condensed
1 pkg. (8 oz.) cream cheese, cut into blocks
2 tbsp. unflavored gelatin
1/2 cup water
1 cup mayonnaise
2 cups boiled shrimp, peeled, deveined, and chopped
1 1/2 cups green onions, chopped
1/2 cup bell peppers, finely diced
2 cloves garlic, crushed and finely minced
1/2 cup celery, finely minced
1 tsp. Cajun Seasoning Mix (see index)
1 tsp. Tabasco® Sauce
Shortening or butter for lightly greasing mold pan
Parsley used as garnish
Crackers or French bread

In a medium saucepan over low-medium heat, add the soup and cream cheese and let the cheese melt into the soup. Use a wire whisk to make sure all the cheese has blended into the soup. In a small bowl, mix the gelatin with the water and stir until the gelatin has dissolved. Add the dissolved gelatin to the soup mixture. Remove from the heat and add the mayonnaise, using the wire whisk to blend it in. Add all the remaining ingredients except for the parsley and whip together with the whisk until well blended.

Return to the heat and cook, stirring constantly, for 3 minutes. Pour into a lightly greased mold pan and refrigerate overnight. Remove carefully from the mold; loosen the sides with a small knife and turn onto a serving plate. Garnish with parsley and serve with crackers or French bread. Serves 10 to 12.

Lagniappe: A great appetizer, party food, or side salad served on top of shredded lettuce. You can make up to 3 days in advance and refrigerate. Let it stay in the mold until you are ready to serve. You can also freeze this dish, which makes it wonderful for planning party food. Just let it thaw completely in the refrigerator before unmolding. You can also use this recipe to make a tasty Lump Crabmeat Mold or Crawfish Mold by substituting lump crabmeat or crawfish for the shrimp. All are excellent versions of a delectable treat.

CHICKEN SALAD

2 whole chicken breasts, with ribs and bones
1 tsp. Cajun Seasoning Mix (see index)
4 large eggs, boiled in their shells
1$\frac{1}{2}$ cups mayonnaise
$\frac{1}{2}$ cup celery, minced
$\frac{1}{2}$ cup green onions, minced
$\frac{1}{4}$ cup bell peppers, finely diced
$\frac{1}{2}$ cup sweet pickle relish
2 tbsp. pimento, chopped
$\frac{2}{3}$ cup toasted pecans, chopped
$\frac{1}{8}$ cup fresh parsley, minced
1 tsp. Tabasco® Sauce
$\frac{1}{2}$ tsp. salt
$\frac{1}{2}$ tsp. black pepper, freshly ground
Crackers, bread, or scooped-out tomato or avocado

Preheat the oven to 400 degrees. Season the 2 chicken breasts with the Cajun Seasoning Mix and bake for 30 minutes. Remove from the oven and let the chicken cool. Remove the skin and debone the chicken; finely chop the chicken and place in a large mixing bowl. Peel the eggs and chop them and add to the bowl with the chicken. Add the remaining ingredients, except for the last one, and blend well. Chill for 30 minutes to let the flavors blend further. Serve on crackers, on bread for sandwiches, or in a scooped-out tomato or avocado. Serves 6.

Lagniappe: This is a chicken salad to remember. I remember my grandmother spending the morning making chicken salad sandwiches to bring to a friend's house for lunch or to serve the family. It makes a wonderful stuffing for an avocado or tomato, becoming a brunch item. You can use this very same recipe and just substitute canned water-packed tuna to make a great Tuna Salad. Don't change anything but the chicken.

CAJUN FRENCH SALAD DRESSING

1/2 cup cider vinegar
1 tsp. Tabasco® Sauce
1 tbsp. brown sugar
1 tbsp. light brown sugar
3 tbsp. chili sauce
1/4 cup catsup
3 cloves garlic, finely minced
1 tsp. salt
1 tsp. sweet basil

1/2 tsp. onion powder
1/2 tsp. garlic powder
1 tbsp. lemon juice, freshly
  squeezed
1/2 tsp. hot dry mustard
1/4 tsp. filé powder
1 large egg, white only
2 cups olive oil, extra virgin

Place the first seven ingredients into a food processor and blend together at high speed until the sugars have dissolved, about 3 minutes. Add the rest of the ingredients except for the salad oil and blend again at high speed for 1 minute.

With the processor on low power, slowly drizzle the oil through the opening at the top into the processor until all the oil has been used. Refrigerate until ready to use. Serve on any green salad. Makes about 3 cups of salad dressing.

Lagniappe: This is a marvelous salad dressing. You can make it ahead of the time you need it and store in the refrigerator up to about a week to keep the flavors at their peak. If you do not have a food processor, you can use a blender or you can mix it by hand using a wire whisk. But be prepared to beat constantly and have a sore arm. This dressing is also great poured on top fresh avocados that have been peeled and sliced.

MAYONNAISE

2 large eggs
1 large egg, yolk only
2 tsp. hot dry mustard
1 tsp. salt
2 tbsp. sugar
2 tbsp. lemon juice

1 tbsp. Worcestershire sauce
1 tsp. Tabasco® Sauce
1 tsp. cider vinegar
$1/2$ tsp. white pepper
$2^1/2$ cups salad oil

Put the first 7 ingredients into a food processor and blend at high speed for 2 minutes. Add the remaining ingredients, except for the salad oil, and blend again for 1 minute. Leave the processor running and remove the opening in the top and slowly drizzle in the salad oil until all is used. Pour into a large quart jar and refrigerate. It will keep safely in the refrigerator for about a week. Makes about 3 cups of mayonnaise.

Lagniappe: There is no comparing this mayonnaise to the mayonnaise you purchase in the store. The flavor of this one is richer and bolder. Use for any recipe that calls for mayonnaise and you will be amazed by the incredible difference fresh mayonnaise makes. You can use this recipe and vary it a bit by adding 3 cloves of crushed garlic to make a wonderful Garlic Mayonnaise. You can also add $1/2$ cup of jalapeno slices to either the Garlic Mayonnaise or to the regular mayonnaise to make Jalapeno Mayonnaise. You can also add flavored vinegars of your choice in place of some or all of the lemon juice to make multiple variations. No matter how you make and serve this dressing, your finished dish will be outstanding.

ROQUEFORT DRESSING

2 cups Mayonnaise (see index)
5 oz. Roquefort cheese,
   crumbled
2 tbsp. onion, minced

$^1/_2$ cup sour cream
$^1/_2$ tsp. onion powder
$^1/_2$ tsp. garlic powder

In a large mixing bowl, mix together all ingredients well with a large, heavy wire whisk. Pour into a quart jar that has a lid and refrigerate for 2 hours before serving. Makes about 3 cups of dressing. Keep refrigerated for up to one week.

Lagniappe: This is the premium salad dressing for any green salad. It is excellent spooned over huge wedges of fresh iceberg lettuce. Roquefort cheese has a distinctive flavor and taste that enhances almost any salad and can be served with almost any meal. You can use this exact recipe to make Blue Cheese Dressing, by substituting blue cheese for the Roquefort cheese in the recipe to make a super Blue Cheese Dressing. You can also use this same recipe to make a Parmesan Cheese Dressing by substituting $^2/_3$ cup of freshly hand-grated Parmesan cheese for the Roquefort cheese. Add 1 tablespoon of sugar and 2 tablespoons of olive oil to the recipe as well.

SEAFOOD

BOILED SHRIMP

1 gal. cold water
2 tbsp. salt
12 whole black peppercorns
5 whole bay leaves
1 large lemon, sliced
1 med. onion, quartered
   (leave the skin on)
2 stalks celery, chopped
3 cloves garlic, crushed
10 whole cloves

$^1/_2$ tsp. dried thyme leaves
$^1/_4$ cup fresh basil, chopped
4 sprigs fresh parsley, whole
2 tbsp. sugar
2 fresh cayenne peppers, cut
   in half (or you can used
   pickled)
2 lbs. fresh shrimp tails,
   unpeeled (21-25's)

In a large stock pot over high heat combine all the ingredients except for the shrimp, and bring to a hard rolling boil. Let the mixture hard boil for 5 minutes, then reduce to a low rolling boil. Add the shrimp. Once the liquid begins to boil again, wait exactly 3 minutes; then turn the heat off. Let the shrimp stand in the liquid for 5 more minutes. Drain the shrimp and serve at once. Serves 4.

Lagniappe: Plain boiled shrimp are great alone. Just cover your table with old newspapers and place the shrimp right in the middle of the table—Cajun style. Serve with a cold, crisp green salad or coleslaw, French bread, and a seafood sauce of your choice. It is simple food at its best.

If you wish to serve the shrimp chilled, drain the hot shrimp and immediately cover the shrimp with ice. Once the shrimp are cold, put them in and airtight container and refrigerate until you are ready to serve. Refrigerated, they will keep nicely for 24 hours. You can hold them for longer, but they begin to lose their quality. Never keep them for more than 2 days.

SHRIMP CREOLE

½ cup cooking oil
2 large onions, coarsely
   chopped
1 large bell pepper, coarsely
   chopped
1 cup celery, chopped
3 cloves garlic, crushed and
   minced
3 cups tomatoes, whole,
   peeled, and chopped
1 tsp. salt
1 tbsp. paprika
1 tsp. Tabasco® Sauce

1 tsp. black pepper
½ tsp. filé powder
1 tsp. sweet basil
½ tsp. thyme
2 large bay leaves
3 lbs. shrimp, peeled and
   deveined (21-25's)
2 tbsp. cornstarch
Enough cold water to dis-
   solve cornstarch
Cooked White Rice (see
   index)

Heat the oil in a large saucepan over medium-high heat until it is hot. Add the onions, bell pepper, celery, and garlic. Sauté until the vegetables are limp and the onions are clear, about 5 minutes. Add the tomatoes and continue to sauté until the tomatoes are slightly browned, about 5 more minutes. Add the salt, paprika, Tabasco® Sauce, black pepper, filé, sweet basil, thyme, and bay leaves and stir in well. Reduce the heat to a simmer for 15 minutes, stirring a few times to prevent any sticking. Add the shrimp and continue to simmer for 10 minutes, stirring often.

To thicken, dissolve the cornstarch in as little cold water as necessary. When dissolved, add to the saucepan and stir it in well. The sauces should thicken quickly. Serve at once over cooked white rice. Serves 6 to 8.

Lagniappe: This dish can be cooked in advance and

refrigerated or frozen for later use. Just do not add the cornstarch before you refrigerate or freeze, as the dish tends to break apart and lose its texture when frozen or refrigerated. Cook up to the point of adding the shrimp and simmer for about 8 of the 10 minutes regular cooking time, then remove from the heat and refrigerate or freeze for later use. To serve, thaw in the refrigerator and when defrosted, add to a saucepan and bring the dish to a low simmer. Then add the cornstarch as directed. This is an easy dish to make, but don't let the ease fool you. It is simply scrumptious.

STUFFED SHRIMP

36 jumbo shrimp (11-15's)
3 tbsp. bacon drippings
1 cup celery, finely chopped
1 cup bell pepper, finely chopped
$1^1/_2$ cups onion, finely chopped
3 cloves garlic, crushed and minced
1 lb. lump crabmeat
$^1/_2$ cup green onions, finely chopped
$^1/_4$ cup fresh parsley, finely chopped
$2^1/_2$ tbsp. flour, all-purpose
2 large eggs, well beaten

1 tsp. Tabasco® Sauce
1 tsp. salt
$^1/_2$ tsp. black pepper
$^1/_2$ tsp. paprika
$^1/_2$ tsp. onion powder
$^1/_8$ tsp. ground bay leaves
$^1/_2$ cup flour, all-purpose
2 tsp. Cajun Seasoning Mix (see index)
2 large eggs, well beaten
1 tbsp. water
1 tsp. Tabasco® Sauce
2 cups French bread crumbs
1 tsp. Cajun Seasoning Mix
3 cups cooking oil

Peel and devein the shrimp, leaving the last segment of shell on the shrimp tail. In a large, heavy skillet, melt the bacon drippings over medium-high heat. Add the celery, bell pepper, onions, and garlic and sauté for 5 minutes, stirring constantly. Add the crabmeat, green onions, and parsley then lower the heat to medium low and sauté for 3 minutes, stirring constantly. Add the $2^1/_2$ tablespoons of flour and blend it in. Remove from the heat and mix in the 2 large eggs, Tabasco® Sauce, salt, black pepper, paprika, onion powder, and bay leaves; blend well together.

Place the shrimp on a flat surface and split the tails in half, cutting down almost through the tail meat but leaving some of the tail meat intact. Spread it open with your fingers and thumbs. Mix the $\frac{1}{2}$ cup of flour and the 2 teaspoons of Cajun Seasoning Mix. Coat each shrimp with the flour mixture. Spoon about 2 tablespoons of the crabmeat stuffing onto each shrimp and mold it on top of the tail. In a medium mixing bowl, mix the 2 eggs, water, and Tabasco® Sauce with a wire whisk, beating them together well. In another mixing bowl, mix the bread crumbs and remaining Cajun Seasoning Mix.

Dip the stuffed shrimp one at a time into the egg mixture, then coat well with the bread crumb mixture. Place on a sheet of waxed paper that has been laid on top of the surface of a large cookie sheet. Repeat the process until all the shrimp are used. When all the shrimp are coated, cover them with another sheet of waxed paper and refrigerate for at least 1 hour. When you are ready to cook the shrimp, pour the oil into a deep-fat fryer or into a large, heavy deep-frying pan and heat the oil to medium high. Fry the shrimp 5 or 6 at a time until they are a golden brown. Remove from the oil and let them drain on layers of dry paper towels. Repeat the process until all the shrimp are cooked. Serve hot. Serves 6 to 8.

Lagniappe: This recipe must be made in advance and refrigerated until you are ready to fry. The stuffed shrimp fry better after being chilled because the stuffing holds together better. You can place them in a 200-degree oven after frying to keep them warm if you like so they will remain uniform in temperature. This is an outstanding company dish. You can do all the preparation in advance and only have to fry the shrimp right before you are ready to serve them. Do not try to reheat the already-fried shrimp; they lose their character and flavor rapidly after cooking and tend to separate or get hard when reheating. You can use this recipe to make Stuffed Crabs by taking the stuffing mixture and either stuffing about 4 tablespoons of the stuffing mixture into the cleaned crab shell tops or using the same amount of mixture onto a foil crab shell. After stuffing, follow the same process of coating the crab shells as you did for each stuffed shrimp tail. Placie the crabs on the cookie sheet covered with wax paper until all the crab shells are stuffed. Fry them the same way you fry the stuffed shrimp, about 4 at a time until golden brown.

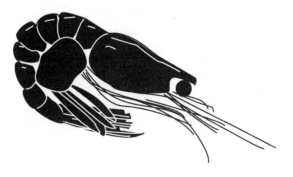

JAMBALAYA AUX CREVETTES (SHRIMP JAMBALAYA)

2 strips bacon, chopped
$^1/_2$ lb. smoked rope sausage, cut into thin circles
2 tbsp. butter, unsalted
1 large onion, chopped
3 cloves garlic, crushed and minced
$^1/_2$ cup celery, minced
1 cup bell pepper, finely chopped
2 large tomatoes, skinned and chopped
1 tsp. chili powder
$^1/_2$ tsp. white pepper
$^1/_2$ tsp. black pepper
$^1/_2$ tsp. cayenne pepper
1 tsp. Tabasco® Sauce
2 cups Seafood Stock or Chicken Stock (see index) or chicken broth
$1^1/_2$ lbs. shrimp, peeled and deveined (21-25's)
$1^1/_2$ tsp. salt
1 cup raw rice, long-grain
$^2/_3$ cup green onions, finely chopped
$^1/_4$ cup parsley, minced

In a large saucepan over medium heat, fry the bacon and sausage until it is brown and crisp. Melt the butter in the saucepan, then add the onion, garlic, celery, and bell pepper; sauté for 5 minutes, stirring constantly. Add the tomatoes and sauté for 3 minutes. Add the chili powder, white pepper, black pepper, cayenne pepper, and Tabasco® Sauce and mix well.

Add the stock, shrimp, salt, and rice. Mix very well, then cover and heat until the dish comes to a boil. Lower the heat to a slow simmer and cook, covered, for 20 minutes. Reduce the heat to a very low heat and let the dish stand for 15 minutes, covered. Then add the green onions and parsley and mix well. Cover and let the jambalaya stand for 5 more minutes on very low heat. Serve hot. Serves 6.

Lagniappe: You can make this dish in advance and

78

refrigerate for up to 3 days until you are ready to serve. You can also freeze it without much loss of texture and quality. To serve, just thaw in the refrigerator and heat it over very low heat until it is warm. Be sure to stir the dish often to prevent sticking. You can also place the jambalaya in a baking dish and heat it, covered, at 325 degrees for about 15 to 20 minutes until it is warm enough to serve.

To make Jambalaya aux Ecrevisses (Crawfish Jambalaya) just substitute 1 pound of crawfish for the shrimp in the recipe above. You can also make Jambalaya aux Crabes (Crab Jambalaya) by substituting 1 pound of lump crabmeat or claw meat for the crawfish and $\frac{1}{2}$ pound of diced ham for the sausage in the recipe above. While they are all jambalaya, the taste of each is uniquely different and exciting.

CRAWFISH ETOUFFEE

1 stick butter, unsalted
1 large onion, chopped
$^1/_2$ cup celery, chopped
1 med. bell pepper, chopped
4 cloves garlic, mashed then
  minced
1 lb. crawfish tails, peeled
1 tsp. salt
1 tsp. black pepper

$^1/_2$ tsp. white pepper
1 tsp. Tabasco® Sauce
1 tsp. onion powder
2 tbsp. flour, all-purpose
$^1/_2$ to 1 cup Seafood Stock
  (see index) or water
$^2/_3$ cup green onions, minced
$^1/_4$ cup fresh parsley, minced
Cooked White Rice (see index)

In a large skillet over medium heat, melt the butter. When
the butter is melted, add the onions, celery, bell pepper,
and garlic and sauté until the onions are limp and clear,
about 5 minutes, stirring constantly. Add the crawfish tails
and season with the salt, black pepper, white pepper,
Tabasco® Sauce, and onion powder. Blend well and cook
over medium heat for 3 minutes. Add the flour and blend
in well, stirring constantly to prevent the flour from sticking to the skillet.

When the flour is blended well, cook it, stirring constantly for 4 minutes. Slowly add the seafood stock, a little at a time, until the sauce is at the consistency of a
thick gravy. Reserve the unused stock for possible later
use. Let the dish cook for about 20 minutes, stirring
often to prevent any sticking. About 3 minutes before
the cooking process is complete, add the green onions
and parsley. Stir in well and cook for the remaining 3
minutes. Adjust the liquid if necessary by using the
reserved stock and serve hot over cooked white rice.
Serves 6.

Lagniappe: There is no doubt that this dish is best when the crawfish are just cooked, but it does refrigerate well for up to 2 days. It can also be frozen with excellent results. You should completely finish the dish before freezing or you can freeze any leftovers in a tightly covered container. To reheat, just thaw in the refrigerator and heat over a low simmer until the dish is hot.

You can use this same recipe to make Crab Étouffée by substituting 1 pound of all-lump crabmeat for the crawfish in this recipe and substituting red bell pepper for the green. You can also use this recipe to make Shrimp Étouffée by substituting $1^{1}/_{2}$ pounds of peeled and deveined shrimp (21-25's) for the crawfish and adding $^{1}/_{2}$ cup of diced canned tomatoes when you add the shrimp to the dish and cook as above. No matter which seafood you choose, étouffée is great Cajun eating!

CRAWFISH STEW

$^1/_2$ cup cooking oil
$^1/_2$ cup flour, all-purpose
2 med. onions, chopped
1 med. bell pepper, chopped
1 cup celery, chopped
3 cloves garlic, minced
2 lbs. crawfish tails, peeled (with their fat if they are fresh)
$1^1/_2$ tsp. salt

1 tsp. Tabasco® Sauce
1 tsp. black pepper
1 cup Seafood Stock (see index) or water
$^2/_3$ cup green onions, minced
$^1/_4$ cup fresh parsley, minced
1 tbsp. lemon juice, freshly squeezed
Cooked White Rice (see index)

Make a roux with the cooking oil and flour over medium heat in a heavy saucepan. Stir the flour until is a dark reddish brown, stirring constantly to prevent sticking with a flexible wire whisk. When the flour is dark reddish brown, add the onions, bell pepper, celery, and garlic and sauté the vegetables for 5 minutes, stirring constantly. Add the crawfish, salt, Tabasco® Sauce, and black pepper and cook for 3 minutes, stirring often. Add the stock or water and blend in well, then reduce the heat to low medium and let the dish begin to simmer lightly. Cover and cook for 15 minutes, stirring a few times while cooking.

Uncover and add the green onions, parsley and lemon juice. Cook for about 5 to 7 more minutes uncovered until the stew is the consistency you like. (Note: There will be a difference in the stew's consistency every time you make this dish, because of the crawfish; some give off more liquid than others, but you can adjust that during the final cooking.) Serve hot over cooked white rice. Serves 8.

Lagniappe: This dish may be made in advance and refrigerated for later use. You can store in the refrigerator for up to 3 days before using. In fact, like all dishes made with a roux, it has a tendency to taste better when made in advance because the roux intensifies with age. You can also freeze for use at a later date. When you are ready to use, thaw in the refrigerator and heat over low heat until the dish begins to simmer and is heated throughout.

You can also use this same recipe to make Shrimp Stew by substituting $2^1/_2$ pounds of peeled and deveined (21-25's) shrimp for the crawfish. I often like to put $^2/_3$ cup of stewed tomatoes into the roux after the vegetables have sautéed and cook the tomatoes for 3 more minutes before adding the shrimp. With or without the tomatoes is a personal choice. The dish is excellent either way. Some restaurants in Louisiana serve shrimp or crawfish stew and call it étouffée, but the taste is dramatically different! Both are excellent, but they are quite different in taste. Both use a roux, but étouffée should not use the dark brown roux!

CAJUN BOILED CRAWFISH

25 lbs. live crawfish
Water to cover and purge
2 cups salt
$^1/_4$ cup soda
6 gal. water
4 lbs. med. red potatoes,
    unpeeled and cleaned
10 small white onions,
    cleaned and unpeeled
10 small whole carrots,
    trimmed
2 lbs. andouille sausage, cut
    into 3-inch links (or any
    spicy sausage)
4 whole cayenne peppers, cut
    in half

4 large lemons, sliced
6 large whole bay leaves
1 bunch fresh parsley
6 stalks celery, cut in thirds
20 cloves garlic, peeled and
    crushed
10 whole allspice
30 whole black peppercorns
$1^1/_2$ cups salt
1 cup dark brown sugar
$^1/_4$ cup Tabasco® Sauce
1 cup cider vinegar
12 ears fresh corn on the cob,
    tips cut and cleaned

First you need to purge the crawfish. In a large tub, add the live crawfish and cover them with tap water. Add the salt and soda and let the crawfish sit in the water for 30 minutes to purge them of their impurities. While the crawfish are purging, add all the remaining ingredients except the corn to a large wire insert that has two handles and place it in a stock pot, gumbo pot, or crawfish boiling pot (about 20-gallon size). Bring the water to a boil over an outdoor boiling setup or crawfish burner. Let the water come to a hard boil, then reduce the heat to a low rolling boil and boil together for 20 minutes.

Add the purged crawfish to the boiling water, turn the heat back up, and bring the pot back to a hard boil. When a hard boil is reached, reduce the heat again to a low rolling boil. Boil the crawfish for 7 minutes, then add the corn and continue to boil for 15 more minutes. Turn the heat down and carefully remove the wire basket and let it drain. Pour the contents onto an outdoor table that has been covered with old newspapers. Serve at once. Serves 6 to 8.

Lagniappe: If you plan to make more than one batch, you can pour the crawfish and vegetables into a large ice chest and close the top. The crawfish will keep warm until you are ready to serve. You can use the remaining boiling water. Just add a new set of ingredients, except for the salt. Add only ²/₃ cup of salt to the water along with all the other ingredients listed above.

You can purge another 25 pounds of crawfish while the first batch is cooking. Purge according to directions above, then continue the cooking process as above. If you are serving 15 to 20 people, you should cook the first batch, then begin the second. When the second batch is done, pour it into the ice chest and begin a new third batch. You can start serving at this time. You'll have enough to get started and when the third batch is cooked, you should have enough for anyone wanting more.

Try to find cardboard trays in which to serve the crawfish and vegetables. You can get those boxes from cola companies or stores that sell cola. As you can tell, this is a complete dinner. If you like, you can serve a nice green salad or coleslaw with the meal.

You can use this same recipe to cook crabs and make Cajun Boiled Crabs by substituting 7 dozen large, fresh live crabs for the crawfish. Follow the process exactly as above, including the purging of the crabs. Serve both crawfish and crabs with either Cocktail Sauce or a sauce made of a recipe for Cocktail Sauce and 1 cup of mayonnaise, blended well together. This sauce is called Cajun

Dipping Sauce for Seafood. It can be made in advance and refrigerated for later use. It will store in the refrigerator for 5 days.

Crawfish boils and crab boils are meant to be party occasions. Be sure to invite friends over for the whole experience. When you think of gathering events, this is a great way to get friends and family over to experience the bounty of the bayous!

QUICK CRAWFISH JAMBALAYA

$^1/_4$ cup peanut oil
1 stick butter, unsalted, cut
   into pieces
1 lb. crawfish tails
2 tbsp. celery, minced
2 tbsp. carrots, finely minced
1 whole shallot, finely minced
1 bunch green onions,
   chopped
2 med. bell pepper, chopped
2 med. fresh tomatoes, sliced
   into wedges

10 large fresh mushrooms,
   sliced
$2^1/_2$ cups Cooked White Rice
   (see index)
$1^1/_2$ tsp. Cajun Seasoning Mix
   (see index)
1 tsp. Tabasco® Sauce
2 tsp. Worcestershire sauce
$^1/_2$ cup dry white wine
$^1/_2$ cup toasted pecan halves
$^1/_2$ cup fresh parsley, minced

In a large, heavy skillet, heat the peanut oil over medium-high heat until it begins to smoke. Add the butter and let it melt, then add the crawfish tails, celery, carrots, and shallots and let them sauté for 3 minutes. Add the green onions and bell pepper and mix well and sauté for 3 more minutes. Add the tomatoes and mix in well; sauté for 1 minute then add the mushrooms and sauté for 1 more minute. Add the rice, Cajun Seasoning Mix, Tabasco® Sauce, Worcestershire sauce, and wine; stir in until the rice is completely mixed and coated with the pan liquids. Add the pecans and parsley and mix in very well. Serve at once. Serves 8.

Lagniappe: This dish is a quick jambalaya that is made to be served right after cooking. You can prepare all the ingredients together before you begin and cook quickly before serving. It is best to chop every thing beforehand and have it lined up to use since this dish is quickly cooked. It is a great one-dish meal. Serve it with hot French bread and a fruit salad with poppy seed dressing.

Use this same recipe to make Quick Shrimp Jambalaya. Just substitute $1^1/_3$ pounds of peeled and deveined shrimp (21-25's). Then follow the recipe as above except add 3 more minutes sautéing time after adding the shrimp, making sure you constantly stir while sautéing. This step is necessary since the crawfish are basically cooked and the shrimp are totally raw.

Use this same recipe to make Quick Crab Jambalaya. Just substitute 1 pound of all-lump crabmeat instead of the pound of crawfish. Follow the recipe as shown. This is a great crab treat that will let you experience the jumbo lumps of crabmeat since the cooking process won't tear the crabmeat apart.

Finally, you can also add 1 pound of smoked sausage cut into 1-inch pieces to give the jambalaya a smoky taste. Just add the sausage before you add the seafood. Sauté it for 5 minutes before you add the seafood and follow as directed above.

SEAFOOD

FRIED CRAWFISH TAILS

2 large eggs, well beaten
2/3 cup milk
2 tbsp. yellow prepared
   mustard
1 tbsp. red wine vinegar
1 tsp. Tabasco® Sauce
1 tsp. salt
1 tsp. fresh ground black
   pepper
1/2 tsp. cayenne pepper

1 lb. crawfish tails, peeled
2 cups flour, all-purpose
1 tbsp. corn starch
1 tsp. baking powder
1 tsp. Cajun Seasoning Mix
   (see index)
1/2 tsp. onion powder
1/2 tsp. cayenne pepper
1/2 tsp. salt
Cooking oil for deep-fat frying

In a large mixing bowl, mix together the eggs, milk, mustard, vinegar, Tabasco® Sauce, salt, black pepper, and cayenne pepper until well blended. Add the pound of crawfish tails and separate them until they are all covered with the batter. Let them soak in the batter for 30 minutes.

Preheat the cooking oil to 375 degrees. In another mixing bowl, mix together the remaining ingredients except for the cooking oil and completely blend well. When you are ready to serve, dip a handful of crawfish at a time into the flour mixture and drop them carefully into the pre-heated cooking oil. Fry them until they come to the surface of the fryer and become a golden brown. Remove with a slotted spoon and put on a layer of dry paper towels in a large platter. Repeat the process until all the crawfish are cooked. Serve hot. Serves 4.

Lagniappe: Eating this dish is almost like eating Cajun Popcorn. The crawfish are so light and tasty you can eat them by themselves or serve them with Cocktail Sauce,

Tartar Sauce or Cajun Dipping Sauce for Seafood (see index). Fried Crawfish also make great po-boys. Just add a handful to $^1/_3$ loaf of fresh French bread spread with Tartar Sauce, lettuce, tomatoes, and pickles and you have a great Crawfish Po-Boy!

You can also use this same recipe for Fried Shrimp by substituting $1^1/_2$ pounds of shrimp, peeled and deveined (21-25's). Just follow the recipe as above. The shrimp will take a little longer to fry, but you still remove them when they are a golden brown. Serve the shrimp the same way you serve the crawfish. You can make Shrimp Po-Boys just like you made the crawfish ones. Both are delicious and easy to make.

CRABMEAT AU GRATIN

1 stick butter, unsalted
1 large onion, minced
$^{1}/_{2}$ cup celery, minced
2 cloves garlic, minced
$^{1}/_{2}$ cup bell pepper, minced
$^{1}/_{2}$ cup flour, all-purpose
1 can (13 oz.) evaporated
  milk
$^{1}/_{4}$ cup heavy whipping cream
3 large eggs, well beaten
1 tsp. salt
1 tsp. Tabasco® Sauce
$^{1}/_{2}$ tsp. white pepper
$^{1}/_{2}$ tsp. black pepper, freshly
  ground
1 lb. crabmeat, jumbo all-lump
$^{1}/_{2}$ cup Swiss cheese, grated
2 tbsp. pimento, diced
2 tbsp. fresh parsley, minced
$^{1}/_{4}$ cup green onion tops,
  minced
1 cup American cheese, grated
Butter to grease baking
  dish(es)
$1^{1}/_{2}$ cups sharp Cheddar
  cheese, grated

Preheat the oven to 375 degrees. In a large, heavy saucepan over moderate heat, add the butter and let it melt. When the butter has melted, sauté the onion, celery, garlic, and bell pepper until the vegetables have wilted and the onions are clear, about 5 minutes. Blend in the flour well until all the liquid is absorbed. Cook for 3 minutes, stirring constantly. Remove from the heat, add the evaporated milk and blend in well.

In another small mixing bowl, combine the whipping cream, eggs, salt, and Tabasco® Sauce until well blended. Return the flour/milk mixture to the heat and reduce the temperature to low. Slowly add a little of the flour mixture to the egg mixture and blend it together. Repeat this process until you have added about 1 cup of flour mixture to the egg mix. Pour the egg mixture into the skillet and stir well until blended and smooth. Add the white and black pepper and mix it in well. Cook the mixture over low heat for 5 minutes. Carefully add the crabmeat, Swiss cheese, pimento, parsley, green onions, and American cheese and blend together, taking care not to tear the lumps of crabmeat.

Pour the crab mixture into 6 lightly greased individual au gratin dishes or a shallow 2-quart casserole. Cover with the grated Cheddar cheese and bake at 375 for 15 minutes or until the casserole is a golden brown. Serve hot. Serves 6.

Lagniappe: You may make this dish in advance and refrigerate for up to 3 days before serving. You can also freeze it either before or after baking. If you freeze it after baking, be sure to cover tightly. To reheat, thaw in the refrigerator until defrosted, then bake at 325 degrees for 15 minutes. To freeze before baking, do not add the Cheddar cheese. Freeze, wrapped well. To serve, thaw in the refrigerator, top with the Cheddar cheese, and bake at 375 degrees for 15 minutes as above.

Use this same recipe to make Crawfish au Gratin. Just substitute 1½ pounds of crawfish tails for the pound of crabmeat and proceed as above, just add 5 minute cooking time. Serve with a green salad and plenty of hot French bread. As another way to serve this dish, you can use small individual pie shells and bake them with the crabmeat or crawfish au gratin in them and serve as a luncheon item or an appetizer. Au gratin gets its name from the crust on top of the dish. It almost always has cheese in the sauce, but an au gratin is something that has a baked crust on top.

FRIED OYSTERS

2 tsp. Cajun Seasoning Mix
   (see index)
$^1/_2$ cup flour, all-purpose
$^1/_4$ tsp. baking soda
$^1/_2$ tsp. baking powder
1 tsp. cornstarch
2 doz. large fresh oysters

2 large eggs, well beaten
1 tsp. Tabasco® Sauce
1 tsp. Worcestershire sauce
1 cup plain dry bread crumbs
$^1/_2$ cup cornmeal
Cooking oil for deep frying

Preheat the oil to 375 degrees in a deep-fat fryer. Mix the first teaspoon of Cajun Seasoning Mix with the flour, baking soda, baking powder, and cornstarch in a large shallow bowl until well blended. Dredge the oysters in the flour mixture one at a time and place them on a plate when finished. Combine the eggs, Tabasco® Sauce, and Worcestershire sauce in another bowl and beat together well. Combine the bread crumbs, cornmeal, and the remaining teaspoon of Cajun Seasoning Mix until well blended. Dip the oysters one at a time into the egg mixture, then roll them in the breadcrumb mixture. Deep fry the oysters in 375-degree oil until they are a golden brown. Remove from the oil and drain on dry paper towels. Serve at once. Serves 2 to 3.

Lagniappe: There is no way to make this in advance. Fried oysters must be eaten right away, just after being cooked. You can double or triple the recipe if you are cooking for a larger number. Take care not to overcook the oysters. As soon as they are a golden brown and very plump, remove them from the oil. Serve with Cocktail Sauce, Tartar Sauce, or with the Cajun Dipping Sauce for Seafood (see index). Use this fried oyster recipe to make a delicious

Oyster Po-Boy. Use $^1/_3$ loaf of fresh French bread. Cover it with Tartar Sauce (see index), dress it with shredded lettuce, tomato slices, and some dill pickle slices, and top with 4 or 5 fried oysters. Talk about heaven!

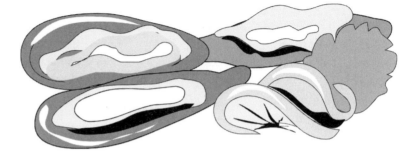

CATFISH COURT BOUILLION

$^1/_2$ cup cooking oil
$^1/_2$ cup flour, all-purpose
1 large onion, chopped
1 large bell pepper, chopped
1 cup celery, chopped
4 cloves garlic, minced
5 cups Seafood Stock (see
  index) or use water
$2^1/_2$ lbs. catfish fillets

1 tsp. salt
1 tsp. black pepper
1 tsp. red pepper
1 tsp. Tabasco® Sauce
$^1/_4$ cup parsley, minced
2 cups tomato sauce
Adjust seasonings to taste
Cooked White Rice
  (see index)

In a large, heavy pot, heat the oil over medium heat until hot. Add the flour and stir constantly, cooking until the flour is a golden brown color. Do not make a dark brown roux. It should be golden brown. Add the onion, bell pepper, celery, and garlic and sauté for 5 minutes, stirring constantly. Add the stock, reduce the heat to low, and let the court bouillion simmer for 30 minutes, covered, stirring a few times.

In a mixing bowl, add the salt, black pepper, and cayenne and blend together well. Season the catfish fillets and drop the fish into the pot with the Tabasco® Sauce, parsley, and tomato sauce. Cook over low heat, stirring a few times for 20 minutes. Check the seasonings for taste and adjust as necessary. Serve over cooked white rice. Serves 6 to 8.

Lagniappe: This is a quick catfish stew that Cajuns are famous for. It can be eaten over rice or served in a soup bowl with rice added. No matter how it is served, it is simply good eating. It's hard to believe that something so easy to make can taste so good. This is the Cajun way to make peoper French Court Bouillion. Sometimes you'll find it called "coubillion" in Cajun country. No matter how it is spelled it's great food.

You can use redfish fillets to make a Redfish Court Bouillion by substituting $2^1/_2$ pounds of redfish fillets for the catfish. When you use the redfish, you can cook the court bouillion for 30 minutes after adding the fish. It will give you a much richer-tasting sauce than the dish made with catfish.

This recipe also does better with wild catfish than the farm-raised ones sold in most of the state. The wild fish has a firmer flesh and can be cooked for up to 40 minutes over low heat. Of course, this will yield a much tastier dish since more of the catfish flavor will find its way into the sauce.

SEAFOOD

FRIED CATFISH

5 lbs. catfish fillets
$^1/_2$ cup prepared yellow mustard
$^1/_4$ cup Tabasco® Sauce
2 tbsp. Worcestershire sauce
$^1/_4$ cup half and half cream
$^1/_2$ cup water
3 tbsp. dry white wine

2 cups white cornmeal
2 cups flour, all-purpose
3 tsp. salt
2 tsp. black pepper
1 tsp. cayenne pepper
1 tsp. onion powder
Cooking oil to deep-fat fry
  the fish

Preheat the oil in a deep-fat fryer to 375 degrees. Cut the fish into 2- to 3-ounce pieces. Combine mustard, Tabasco® Sauce, Worcestershire sauce, cream, water, and wine in a large mixing bowl until well blended. Put the white cornmeal in a food processor and blend at high speed for 3 minutes. It will make the mixture much finer. Pour the mixture into another large, dry mixing bowl and add the flour and remaining ingredients except for the cooking oil. Mix well together with a flexible wire whisk until well blended. Coat the fish pieces in the mustard mixture, then roll the fish in the dry cornmeal mixture.

Fry the fish in a deep-fat fryer at 375 degrees. The fish should float to the top of the grease and turn a golden brown. Remove from the fryer and drain on a stack of dry paper towels. Serve with French fries and coleslaw. Serve hot. Serves 6 to 8.

Lagniappe: Fried catfish is truly a work of culinary art. The fish is almost made to be deep-fat fried. It is so light and tender and so delicious. It doesn't take long to cook and the results are remarkable. A fish fry is another opportunity for the community to come together. It allows for a large gathering of people to come together and celebrate good eating and good friends. It's the Cajun way . . . almost any excuse to have a party!

FROG LEGS SAUCE PIQUANTE

1¼ cups peanut oil
1 cup flour, all-purpose
4 med. onions, chopped
5 cloves garlic, minced
1 cup celery, chopped
1 large bell pepper, chopped
1 whole cayenne pepper, finely chopped
3 cans (15 oz. ea.) stewed tomatoes
4 cups Seafood Stock(see index) or use chicken broth
1 cup dry white wine
1 tsp. garlic powder

1 tsp. onion powder
1 tsp. black pepper, freshly ground
½ tsp. white pepper
1 tsp. Tabasco® Sauce
1 tbsp. Worcestershire sauce
2 tbsp. lemon juice, freshly squeezed
2 tbsp. peanut oil
18 large frog legs, cleaned and skinned
2 tsp. Cajun Seasoning Mix (see index)
Cooked White Rice (see index)

In a large saucepan over medium-high heat, add the peanut oil and heat it until it is hot and begins to smoke. Add the flour and cook, stirring constantly, until the roux becomes a dark brown. It should be the color of fudge, but take care not to let the roux stick or it will burn and become very bitter. Add the onions, garlic, celery, bell pepper, and cayenne pepper and sauté for 5 minutes in the roux over medium heat. Add the solid pieces from the stewed tomatoes, reserving the liquid for later use.

Sauté for 5 minutes or until the tomato pieces start to dissolve into the roux. Add the stock and white wine and blend together until the sauce becomes smooth. Add the seasonings, Tabasco® Sauce, Worcestershire sauce and lemon juice and blend in well. Bring the liquid to a boil, then reduce it to a low simmer and cook covered for 1 hour, stirring a few times to make sure no sticking is taking place.

In a heavy skillet over medium heat, add the 2 table-spoons of peanut oil and heat until hot. Season the frog legs evenly with the Cajun Seasoning Mix, rubbing the seasoning into the meat with your fingers. Fry the frog legs 4 or 5 at a time, until they are a nice golden brown on all sides. Remove to a warm plate until all the legs are browned, then set them aside for later use. When the sauce has cooked for 1 hour, add the browned frog legs and stir them into the sauce. Continue to simmer for 3 more hours, covered, over a low simmering heat. Serve hot over cooked white rice. Serves 6 to 8.

Lagniappe: This is an excellent dish that is very popular in all of Acadiana. It can be made in advance and stored in the refrigerator for up to 4 days. In fact, this storage seems to improve the flavor of the dish and allow the flavors to completely blend together. It can also be frozen without any harm to the quality of the dish. To reheat, just thaw in the refrigerator and heat over low heat until the sauce is hot and the frog legs are heated through.

You can also use this recipe with a few modifications to make Rabbit Sauce Piquante, another famous Louisiana Cajun dish. Just substitute 2 medium rabbits (about 3 pounds each) for the frog legs. Cut the rabbit into serving pieces and season and fry as you would the frog legs. Change the Seafood Stock to Chicken Stock (see index) or use chicken broth. You will need 2 more tablespoons of peanut oil to fry the rabbit and 1 more teaspoon of Cajun Seasoning Mix to season the meat. The rest of the recipe remains intact.

Use this recipe to make Squirrel Sauce Piquante by making the following changes: Use whole, skinned, and cleaned squirrels for the frog legs. Use 1 extra teaspoon of Cajun Seasoning Mix to season the squirrel. Use 2 more tablespoons of peanut oil to fry the squirrel and use Beef Stock (see index) instead of Seafood Stock. Sauce piquante is a favorite no matter what meat is used.

These three wild meats make outstanding Sauce Piquante because they all hold up to the long cooking time and flavor the sauce with the goodness of the meat used. Both rabbit and squirrel hunting are favorite pastimes of Cajun men. Of course, Cajuns don't kill anything that they don't plan on eating! All three dishes are popular. The one you get depends on the answer to the question: "Mais, what kinda meat you got, cher?"

PAN–CRUSTED REDFISH

4 fillets (12 oz. ea.) redfish
$^1/_2$ stick butter, unsalted,
   melted
1 tsp. Tabasco® Sauce
3 tbsp. Cajun Seasoning Mix
   (see index)

4 tbsp. butter, unsalted, cut
   into 4 pats
4 tbsp. butter, unsalted,
   melted

Check each redfish fillet to be sure that there are no bones remaining. Combine the $^1/_2$ stick of melted butter with the Tabasco Sauce in a shallow pan. Dip the fillets into the butter mixture. Remove and sprinkle them generously with equal amounts of the Cajun Seasoning Mix, rubbing the seasoning into the fish with your fingers.

Place a very heavy metal skillet over high heat and allow it to get very hot. Add one of the 1-tablespoon pats of butter to the pan, then add a fillet of fish to the skillet. Let the fish cook for 2 minutes, then flip it over to the other side. Add 1 tablespoon of the melted butter over the fish. This will cause a great deal of smoke, so be sure that the fan on your stove works well. Better yet, cook the fish outside over a butane burner (crawfish burner). It will give you the heat that you need, but it will not smoke up your house. Also, keep in mind that the skillet could catch fire because of the high temperature and the addition of the liquid butter. Cook this side of the fish for 2 more minutes, then remove the fish to a warm platter.

When the fillet is cooked and out of the skillet, carefully wipe the skillet with a few paper towels to remove the butter and as much of the seasoning as possible. Repeat the process for the second fillet and continue until all the fillets are cooked. If you have a large enough skillet, you can cook two fillets at a time, which helps speed the process. Just be sure to add the proper amount of butter to the skillet each time. Place the cooked fillet on the warm platter and put into a 175-degree oven to keep it warm until you are ready to serve. Serve the fish hot with a little melted butter. Serves 4.

Lagniappe: This is not a make-ahead dish. You have to eat it right after it is cooked. It will keep at 175 degrees for about 30 minutes, but should be eaten right after all the fillets are cooked. Be sure to wear something to protect your clothing while you are cooking, since this dish does tend to spatter and smoke quite a lot. That's why making it out of doors is more appropriate. However, if you have a great vent in your kitchen, you should be okay. I generally cook up to four fillets inside. If I need more than four, I cook outdoors. The fish will be well crusted and have such a delightful flavor.

It will seem like you are putting too much seasoning on the fish, but the fast cooking process and the high heat tend to caramelize the seasonings and create a delightful sensation that is unlike anything you've tasted. Don't be concerned by the appearance of the fish. It will appear that you have burned it, but the taste will tell you differently.

You can use this same recipe to make Pan-Crusted Trout by using trout fillets instead of redfish. You will need to cut the cooking time to 1½ minutes on each side, since the trout will tend to cook faster. You can also make Pan-Crusted Red Snapper by using red snapper fillets in place of the redfish. To cook snapper, just add ½ minute to each side's cooking time. No matter which fish you choose to use, you are in for a genuine treat! *Ça cést boncoup bon!*

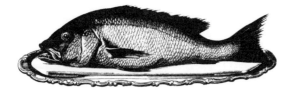

MEATS AND MEAT DISHES

CHAUDIN

1 whole pork stomach
  (chaudin), trimmed
  and cleaned
Water to cover
1 cup red wine vinegar
2 large lemons, cut into circles
$^1/_4$ cup salt
5 whole bay leaves
$^1/_4$ cup baking soda
4 slices bacon, finely chopped
$^1/_2$ stick butter
1 large onion, chopped
1 large bell pepper, finely
  chopped
3 stalks celery, finely minced
5 cloves garlic, finely minced
1 cup green onions, minced
$^1/_2$ cup parsley, minced
$^1/_4$ cup fresh basil, minced
$1^1/_2$ cups mushrooms, sliced
1 lb. pure pork sausage,
  chopped
1 lb. ground beef
1 lb. ham, minced

2 cups French bread, torn
  into pieces
1 cup milk
3 large eggs, well beaten
3 tsp. Cajun Seasoning Mix
  (see index)
$^1/_4$ cup butter, softened
2 cups Beef Stock (see index)
  or use beef broth
1 cup dry red wine
$^1/_2$ cup red wine vinegar
2 large onion, chopped
4 cloves garlic, minced
1 large bell pepper, julienned
3 med. turnips, cut into
  1-inch cubes
4 stalks celery, sliced
1 lb. mushrooms, sliced
2 lbs. new potatoes, washed
  and trimmed
2 tsp. Tabasco® Sauce
2 tbsp. Worcestershire sauce
1 tbsp. fresh basil, minced
$^1/_2$ tsp. oregano

Buy a cleaned pork stomach from your local butcher. Be sure he has thoroughly cleaned it. Place it in a large stock pot and cover it completely with cold water. Add the red wine vinegar, lemon circles, salt, bay leaves, and soda and stir the water to make sure the soda has dissolved. Let the stomach stand for $1^1/_2$ hours. While the stomach is resting, begin to make the stuffing.

MEATS AND MEAT DISHES

In a large heavy skillet, add the bacon pieces and let them fry until they are crisp, stirring often. When they are crisp, add the butter and let it melt. Then sauté the onions, bell pepper, celery, and garlic until the onions are clear, about 5 minutes. Add the green onions, parsley, basil, and mushrooms and sauté for 3 more minutes, stirring constantly. Add the pork sausage, ground meat, and ham and continue to sauté for 10 more minutes or until the ground beef has browned nicely.

While the meats are browning, add the French bread, milk, and egg into a medium-sized mixing bowl and let the bread soak up the liquid. Mash the bread with your hands until it falls apart. Use 2 teaspoons of the Cajun Seasoning Mix to season the meat mixture. Remove from the heat and add the French bread mixture to the meat; blend together until the mixture all looks the same.

Preheat the oven to broil. When the chaudin has finished soaking, remove from the pot and rinse it well under running water. Be sure to wash it thoroughly. Place the chaudin on a large cutting board and using kitchen string, sew together one side until the opening is closed. Using a large kitchen spoon, put the stuffing from the skillet into the chaudin until all is used. It will begin to stretch and enlarge.

When you have used all the stuffing, sew up the other end with the kitchen string, closing it tightly. Season the outside of the chaudin with the remaining 1 teaspoon of Cajun Seasoning Mix and rub it all over with the softened butter. Place the chaudin in a heavy, large black iron pot that has a lid. Put it under the broiler and let it brown nicely on the top. Then turn it so another part can brown. Repeat until all the outside is nice and dark brown. It takes about 5 to 7 minutes under the broiler for each side to brown. Remove from the oven and turn it to 350 degrees and close the door. Add the remaining ingredients to the pot with the chaudin, cover, and return to the oven. Bake covered for $2^1/_2$ to 3 hours.

MEATS AND MEAT DISHES

When the cooking time has finished, remove from the oven and take the chaudin from the pot carefully with two large spoons and place on a large platter. Let the chaudin cool for 5 minutes, then cut it in 1-inch slices. Spread the slices across the platter and spoon the juices and vegetables from the black iron pot on top of the meat. Serve at once. Serves 6 to 8.

Lagniappe: This is a detailed recipe, but it is not difficult. It is a tradition in Cajun culture, especially at butchering times. Today, you have to find a shop that butchers whole pigs to be able to obtain pig stomachs, but finding a source is well worth the trouble. I do have to admit that it is hard to find, and the only time I cook chaudin is on very special occasions and for very special guests. The taste is dramatic, but, alas, so often people will not even give it a chance. I generally don't like to tell guests what it is until they mention how good it is. Then I say it's stuffed chaudin, and let it go at that, since fewer and fewer people speak French today. This is true Cajun fare and fits the traditional Cajun belief in not letting anything go to waste. It is fine Cajun eating at its best. Few people have the opportunity to feast on Chaudin; don't let the chance go by if you have an opportunity to experience this great meal.

MEATS AND MEAT DISHES

STUFFED BELL PEPPERS

4 large bell peppers
Water to cover
1 tbsp. baking soda
2 tbsp. salt
1 stick butter, unsalted
3 tbsp. olive oil, extra virgin
1 large onion, finely chopped
$^2/_3$ cup celery, minced
1 large eggplant, peeled and
   cut into cubes
$^1/_2$ cup bell pepper, chopped
4 cloves garlic, minced
$^1/_4$ cup fresh parsley, minced
$^1/_2$ lb. ground sirloin
$^1/_2$ lb. shrimp, peeled and
   deveined, chopped

$^1/_2$ lb. pure pork sausage,
   finely chopped
3 cups French bread, torn
   into pieces
$^1/_2$ cup milk
3 large eggs
1 tsp. Cajun Seasoning Mix
   (see index)
1 tsp. garlic powder
1 tsp. onion powder
1 tsp. Tabasco® Sauce
$^1/_2$ tsp. cayenne pepper
$^1/_2$ cup seasoned bread
   crumbs

Preheat the oven to 350 degrees. Split the peppers in half, lengthwise. Remove the centers and membranes, wash them, place them in a large saucepan, then cover with water. Add the salt and soda and parboil the peppers over medium heat for 5 minutes. Remove when done and refrigerate in a tightly covered bowl until ready to use.

In a large, heavy skillet, over medium-high heat, add the butter and let it melt. When the butter has melted, add the olive oil and sauté the onions, celery, eggplant, bell pepper, and garlic for 7 minutes over medium heat, stirring constantly. Add the parsley, ground meat, shrimp, and sausage and continue to sauté for 10 more minutes, stirring constantly. In a large bowl, add the French bread and dampen it with the milk. When the milk has been soaked up by the bread, squeeze as much of it as you can from the bread and discard.

Once the milk is discarded, add the eggs and blend in well with the softened French bread. Pour in the sautéed meats and vegetables and blend together well. Season with the remaining ingredients except for the bread crumbs and mix together well. Pour into a baking dish and bake in the oven for 1½ hours at 350 degrees. When done, remove from the oven and let cool for 10 minutes, then tightly cover with plastic wrap and refrigerate for at least 4 hours.

When the time has elapsed and you are ready to stuff the peppers, take the peppers and the stuffing mix from the refrigerator and fill each of the peppers with the chilled stuffing mix. Place on a lightly greased baking sheet and top each pepper with the bread crumbs. Broil about 10 inches from the heat for about 15 minutes or until the peppers are warm and the top is a golden toasted brown. Serve at once. Serves 4 to 8 with either one or two peppers per person.

Lagniappe: This is a wonderful stuffed pepper. It takes a bit of preparation time, but the finished product is well worth it. If you decide to make more stuffed peppers, you can double or triple this recipe without much effort. Just be sure to have a skillet big enough to hold the stuffing mixture. The flavors blend so well in this recipe and create a truly scrumptious stuffed pepper. While this recipe is almost a two-day process, I find that you can make a large batch and freeze some and keep some to eat. This recipe is great for company meals and, except for the time required, is a wonderful treat for a family meal as well. I like to make this dish when the big bell peppers of summer start to appear in the stores or at the farmers' market.

MEATS AND MEAT DISHES

COCHON DE LAIT

1 20-lb. whole young pig
$^1/_4$ cup butter, softened
5 tbsp. Cajun Seasoning Mix
   (see index)
8 cloves garlic
3 med. shallots, quartered
1 tsp. fresh rosemary leaves
8 small tender young turnips

4 small onions, peeled but
   left whole
6 small young carrots, washed
   and trimmed
$^1/_2$ cup dry white wine
1 tsp. Tabasco® Sauce
1 tbsp. Worcestershire sauce

Preheat the oven to 300 degrees. Have the butcher remove the pig's head and feet up to the knee joints. Ask the butcher to split the pig in half with a vertical cut through the entire pig. Be sure to ask him to clean the pig. Rub the softened butter on all of the pig, inside and out, then season well with the Cajun Seasoning Mix. Cut small slits into the meat inside of the pig and stuff them with garlic cloves and quarters of shallots.

Place the pig in a large, heavy baking pan with the hind legs under the pig pointing forward and the front legs down under, pointing back. Sprinkle with the rosemary leaves and arrange the whole turnips, onions, and carrots around the sides of the pig. Mix together the wine, Tabasco® Sauce, and Worcestershire sauce in a small bowl and pour the mixture into the bottom of the baking pan. Place in the oven and bake at 300 degrees for 8 hours. You can baste the pig every hour with the pan drippings.

When the pig has cooked, remove from the oven. Let it cool for 15 minutes, then place on a carving board and carve. If you prefer, you can serve the whole pig on a platter with the baked vegetables surrounding it on the table. Then carve as served. Serves 10 to 12.

Lagniappe: The term *cochon de lait* means suckling pig. In other words, it is still milk fed, so the meat is tender and light. The tradition was to cook the whole pig. Because it was so small, usually 25 to 30 pounds whole, it cooked faster and the meat just fell off the bone. Today, larger pigs are often used, because of the crowds that are attracted to the process. It becomes a reason to have a party. So today, a cochon de lait means a party with a whole pig as the feast. Originally, this dish was cooked over an open fire with the pig on a spit that could be turned. Today, we also use the term to define the cooking of a small whole pig. It's much quicker and less trouble in the oven.

You can still have a party and prepare and serve the whole pig with ambience but with little of the bother of preparing to do the chore outdoors. While this recipe calls for removing the head, if you are adventurous you certainly can leave the head on. Just be sure to have the tongue and eyes removed by the butcher. This is a dish that is made to impress your guests. It takes a while to cook, but the process is not difficult at all.

CORNBREAD DRESSING

2¹/₂ lbs. ground chuck
1 lb. country sausage, hot
1 tbsp. garlic, minced
2¹/₂ cups onions, finely
   chopped
1 cup celery, minced
1¹/₂ cups bell pepper, finely
   chopped
¹/₂ cup carrots, finely minced
2 tsp. Cajun Seasoning Mix
   (see index)
1 tsp. Tabasco® Sauce
1 tbsp. Worcestershire sauce

1 tsp. onion powder
1 tsp. sage
3 cups Chicken Stock (see
   index) or chicken broth
1 can (10³/₄ oz.) cream of
   mushroom soup
1 cup green onion tops,
   minced
¹/₂ cup parsley, minced
3 large eggs, well beaten
5 cups cornbread, crumbled
3 cups French bread, torn
   into small pieces

In a heavy metal skillet over medium-high heat, add the ground chuck and country sausage and sauté until they are nicely browned. Add the onions, celery, bell pepper, and carrots and sauté for 5 minutes, stirring constantly. Add the Cajun Seasoning Mix, Tabasco® Sauce, Worcestershire sauce, onion powder, and sage, blend together well, and cook for 1 minute. Add the stock, lower the heat to a low simmer, and simmer for 1 hour, stirring occasionally to prevent sticking.

After the meat has simmered for 1 hour, add the mushroom soup, green onions, parsley, eggs, cornbread, and French bread. Blend together until completely mixed. Place the dressing in a lightly greased baking dish and bake for 30 minutes at 325 degrees. Serve hot. Serves 8 to 10.

Lagniappe: This cornbread dressing is as good as it gets. You can serve it as a side dish, eat it as a meal in itself (I like it hot or cold), or use it as a stuffing for your turkey, chicken, or duck. This dressing is a holiday feast in itself. If you are looking for something to bring to a buffet or a party, this will be quite a hit. Don't look at the ingredient list to determine if this dish is hard to make. Read the directions. It is simple cooking and delectable eating! This recipe is a version that my mother used to make for every holiday meal. It goes well with whatever meat you decide to serve.

DAUBE

1 large (5 to 6 lbs.) roast, beef shoulder
6 cloves garlic, cut in half
1 med. shallot, cut into 8 pieces
1 whole cayenne pepper, cut into 6 pieces
$^{1}/_{2}$ pound andouille sausage, cut into small pieces
2 tsp. Cajun Seasoning Mix (see index)
$^{1}/_{2}$ cup vegetable oil
$^{1}/_{2}$ cup flour, all-purpose

2 large onions, chopped
2 large bell peppers, chopped
1 cup celery, minced
2 tbsp. garlic, minced
1 cup carrots, minced
1 cup stewed tomatoes
1 cup dry red wine
1 tsp. Tabasco® Sauce
2 cups Beef Stock (see index)
$^{1}/_{2}$ cup parsley, minced
Adjust seasonings to taste
Cooked White Rice (see index)

Place the roast on a cutting board and cut slits into the meat with a knife. Open holes with your fingers. Stuff garlic, shallot, cayenne, and andouille into the holes. Fill the holes with as much as you can, then make another slit and repeat the process until you use all the stuffing pieces you have. Season the dish well with the Cajun Seasoning Mix. Don't worry about closing the holes. When you brown and sear the roast the holes will close naturally.

In a large, heavy pot that has a lid and is big enough to hold the roast and vegetables, add the vegetable oil and let it get hot. When the oil starts to smoke, add the roast, carefully taking care not to splatter the oil. Brown the roast on all four sides, making sure a dark brown crust starts to form on all sides of the roast.

When the roast is completely brown, remove from the pot and set aside. Add the flour and cook, stirring constantly, until the roux that is made becomes a dark reddish brown, about 12 minutes over medium-high heat.

When that color is reached, quickly add the onions, bell pepper, celery, garlic, and carrots and sauté in the roux for 5 minutes, stirring constantly. Add the tomatoes and sauté for 3 more minutes, mashing the tomatoes as much as possible into the roux. Add the wine, Tabasco® Sauce, and Beef Stock and cook, stirring constantly, until the mixture is smooth. Add the parsley to the liquid and stir it through.

Put the roast back in the pot, cover, reduce the heat and cook for $2^1/_2$ hours or until the roast is very tender. Before serving, sample the juice and adjust seasonings to taste. Slice the roast right in the pot and serve at once over Cooked White Rice. Serves 8 to 10.

Lagniappe: Cooking cheap cuts of meat was a must in Cajun Country. The better pieces of meat were saved for special occasions or perhaps never served. I grew up not knowing that meat could be cooked quickly. I thought you just had to cook for quite a while for meat to be ready. Now the flavor of a pot roast is hard to beat! All the seasoning that went into the roast helped to make this "less than prime cut of meat" seem to be fit for a king.

Cooking meat for a long time brought out its full flavor and made the sauce (gravy) wonderful over rice. This meat may be made in advance and refrigerated for up to 4 days before serving. You can also freeze the Daube with great results. Just thaw in the refrigerator until you are ready to serve and heat either on top of the stove over low heat for 30 minutes, or heat, covered, in the oven at 350 degrees for 30 minutes or until hot.

If you like sandwiches, try a Daube PoBoy or Daube Sandwich! Just slice a generous amount of meat and place on a dressed bun or half a loaf of French bread. Dress with mayonnaise, Creole mustard, lettuce, pickle, and fresh tomatoes. A sandwich made for a king but served to commoners!

MEATS AND MEAT DISHES

STUFFED EGGPLANT

3 med. eggplants
$^1/_4$ tbsp. butter, unsalted
2 large onions, chopped
2 med. bell pepper, chopped
2 cups celery, minced
$^1/_4$ cup garlic, minced
$1^1/_4$ lbs. ground round beef
$1^1/_2$ lbs. shrimp, peeled and
   deveined (41-50's)
$^1/_2$ lb. andouille sausage, finely chopped
2 tsp. Cajun Seasoning Mix
   (see index)
1 tbsp. Worcestershire sauce
1 tsp. Tabasco® Sauce

1 tsp. onion powder
1 tsp. garlic powder
$^1/_2$ tsp. cayenne pepper
1 cup green onions, finely
   chopped
$^1/_2$ cup parsley, minced
$^1/_2$ tsp. sweet basil leaves
2 cups Cooked White Rice
   (see index)
$^1/_2$ cup seasoned bread
   crumbs
2 pats butter, cut into small
   pieces
1 tsp. paprika

Wash the eggplants well and cut off the stems. Place a steamer over medium-high heat, add water to the bottom, and place the 3 eggplants in the steamer. Bring the water to a boil and when it is boiling hard, count 5 minutes, then reduce the heat to a simmer. Let the eggplants steam for 10 minutes, then turn off the heat and let them stay in the steamer.

Preheat the oven to 425 degrees. In a large, heavy skillet over medium-high heat, add the butter and let it melt. When the butter is melted, add the onions, bell pepper, celery, and garlic then sauté for 4 minutes. Add the ground meat and brown over medium heat. Add the shrimp and andouille sausage and cook until the shrimp are pink all the way through, about 10 minutes. Add the seasoning mix, Worcestershire sauce, Tabasco® Sauce, onion powder, garlic powder, and cayenne and mix thoroughly together. Remove the skillet from the heat and set aside for later use.

Remove the eggplants from the steamer. They should be cool enough to handle. Cut each eggplant in half, lengthwise, and scoop the pulp out of the center, leaving about $1/4$ inch of the pulp around the skin on all sides. Place the pulp in a large bowl and mash it with a heavy slotted spoon or a potato masher. Add the pulp to the skillet with the meat and shrimp and blend in well. Add the green onions, parsley, basil, and rice, then mix thoroughly.

Using a large kitchen spoon, fill each of the eggplant shells and place them on a lightly greased baking sheet. Sprinkle them evenly with the bread crumbs and dot with the pieces of butter. Dust with paprika and bake for 30 minutes at 425 degrees. Remove from the oven and serve. Serves 6.

Lagniappe: What can I say? This is easy, quick, pretty, and tasty. It is superb! Eggplant is made to be stuffed with this mixture of meat, shrimp, and sausage, all put together in a Cajun culinary delight. You can make this dish in advance and refrigerate or freeze for later use. You can make and store in the refrigerator up to 3 days, covered with plastic wrap. Completely bake the dish if you are going to freeze it, then wrap it tightly with plastic wrap and freeze. To use, just thaw in the refrigerator and bake at 350 degrees for 15 minutes. You can use this same recipe and substitute all-lump jumbo crabmeat to make a wonderful Crabmeat Stuffed Eggplant. Just substitute $1^1/2$ pounds of all-lump jumbo crabmeat for the shrimp and cancel the ground meat and increase the andouille sausage to 1 pound. Follow the rest of the recipe as printed. No matter which way you fix it, you are in for a real treat!

MEATS AND MEAT DISHES

GRILLADES

1 large (2½ to 3 lbs.) round steak
2½ tsp. Cajun Seasoning Mix (see index)
2 tbsp. cooking oil
2 large onions, chopped
1 large bell pepper, julienned
½ cup celery, minced
3 cloves garlic, minced
1 tbsp. flour, all-purpose
2 cups Beef Stock (see index)
⅔ cup dry red wine
1 tsp. Tabasco® Sauce
1 tbsp. Worcestershire sauce
¼ cup fresh parsley, minced
Cooked White Rice (see index)

Cut the round steak into serving pieces, about 1½ inches wide and 3 inches long. Season well with the Cajun Seasoning Mix. In a heavy metal skillet that has a cover, heat the oil over medium heat. Add the cooking oil and let it get hot. Then brown the steak pieces until they are well browned on both sides, about 5 minutes. Remove the steak to a warm platter and reserve for later use. Add the onions, bell pepper, celery, and garlic and sauté for 5 minutes over medium heat. Sprinkle the flour on top and blend it in well. Cook the flour in the mixture for 3 minutes, stirring constantly.

Add the Beef Stock and blend in well. When the sauce is smooth, return the steak strips to the skillet. Stir well, then cover and reduce the heat to a low simmer and cook for 1 hour, stirring occasionally. Then add the wine, Tabasco® Sauce, and Worcestershire sauce and blend in. Then cover and cook for 40 more minutes over a very low simmer, stirring occasionally. Add the parsley, and blend it in. Serve the grillades and gravy over cooked white rice. Serves 6.

Lagniappe: This is the grillades of Cajun country. It is also made similarly and served over grits in the city (New

MEATS AND MEAT DISHES

Orleans). This version is a bit spicier and just a little bit less formal. This is the only steak I knew growing up. I just thought all steaks were braised like round steak. It wasn't until I was much older that I found out there were many types of steak and many ways to cook them. Of course, since we were from a large family, round steak (grillades) was the only steak we could afford.

Looking back, we weren't deprived, It's hard to beat grillades for taste and tenderness. The gravy made from this slow-cooking technique is out of the world, and the meat can easily be cut with a fork. You'll find grillades across Louisiana in Cajun, Creole, and uptown city homes. This recipe refrigerates well and freezes easily, with great results. To reheat, just simmer over low heat until the dish is hot.

STUFFED PORK CHOPS

4 large (1½ in. thick) pork chops
3½ tsp. Cajun Seasoning Mix (see index)
4 strips bacon, chopped
1 small onion, chopped
½ cup bell pepper, diced
¼ cup celery
3 cloves garlic, minced
3 tbsp. carrot, minced
½ cup mushrooms, finely chopped
2 cups French bread, torn into small pieces
1 large egg, well beaten

¼ cup half and half cream
1 tsp. Tabasco® Sauce
½ cup flour, all-purpose
2½ tsp. cooking oil
2 stalks celery, julienned
4 med. tender young carrots, cleaned and julienned
1 med. onion, julienned
1 large red bell pepper, julienned
1 cup Beef Stock (see index)
1 tsp. Tabasco® Sauce
1 tbsp. Worcestershire sauce
½ cup dry red wine

Preheat the oven to 375 degrees. Season each of the pork chops equally with 2 teaspoons of the Cajun Seasoning Mix. Cut a slit to make a pocket for the stuffing in each of the pork chops. The pocket should be large enough to hold about ⅔ cup of stuffing. After you cut the outside, use your finger to widen the inside pocket. Your slit should be about 1 inch wide but go all the way back to the bone. The inside pocket should be about 3½ inches wide. This will make a nice size pocket for stuffing.

In a heavy, large metal skillet, sauté the bacon until it is brown and crisp. Add the onions, bell pepper, celery, garlic, carrots, and mushrooms and sauté for 5 minutes, stirring constantly. Add the French bread and sauté the bread pieces for 4 more minutes. The bread should brown somewhat. Add 1 teaspoon of the Cajun Seasoning Mix remaining and blend in well. Remove from the heat and add the egg, cream, and Tabasco® Sauce and mix thoroughly until well blended. This will make your stuffing for the chops. Stuff each chop with $1/4$ of the stuffing mix, forcing it into the cavity you created with your knife earlier. In a medium mixing bowl, combine the remaining $1/2$ teaspoon of Cajun Seasoning Mix and the flour. Dredge each pork chop in the seasoned flour.

Clean the skillet with a few dry paper towels and add the cooking oil. Heat the oil over medium-high heat and when the oil is hot, add the 4 stuffed chops to the skillet. Brown each nicely on both sides until a nice brown crust forms on each chop. Remove the chops to a warm platter and reserve for later use. Add the vegetables remaining to the skillet and sauté them for 3 minutes, stirring constantly.

Return the chops to the skillet and place on top of the sautéed vegetables and bake for 20 minutes at 375 degrees uncovered. Reduce the heat to 275 degrees and remove the skillet from the oven. Add the remaining ingredients, cover, and return to the oven. Let the dish cook for $1^1/2$ hours at 275 degrees. Serve hot with the pan drippings and the cooked vegetables. Serves 4.

Lagniappe: This is company eating. You can do everything in advance through the stuffing of the chops. When you are ready to serve, just continue to cook the chops as directed. You can freeze the pork chops after they are stuffed, but do not finish cooking them until you defrost and are ready to serve. I like to make a number of stuffed chops and freeze them in fours to be able to serve when I like. You can also refrigerate after stuffing the chops and wait for up to 3 days before completing the cooking process. This is an oven braise and will make the chops very tender and full of flavor. It makes the chops look like they are about $1^1/2$ pounds each and makes for a beautiful entrée.

MEATS AND MEAT DISHES

As an alternative, you can add oysters to the stuffing, creating a wonderful Pork Chops with Oyster Dressing. Just add 1 cup of oysters to the stuffing mixture as you add the French bread and cook the recipe as above. You might want to have your pork chops cut about 2 inches thick since you'll need a bit more room for the stuffing. A real delight!

MEATS AND MEAT DISHES

STUFFED TURNIPS

8 large, tender young turnips
Water to steam turnips
1 lb. ground round
1 lb. pure pork ground
  sausage (pan style)
$^1/_2$ lb. andouille sausage, finely chopped
1 large yellow onion, chopped
1 large bell pepper, chopped
$^2/_3$ cup celery, minced
5 cloves garlic, minced
3 tsp. Cajun Seasoning Mix
  (see index)

1 tsp. Tabasco® Sauce
$^1/_2$ tsp. garlic powder
1 tbsp. Worcestershire sauce
$1^1/_2$ cups Cooked White Rice
  (see index)
1 cup plain bread crumbs
1 cup green onions, finely
  chopped
$^1/_4$ cup fresh parsley, minced
$^1/_2$ cup seasoned bread
  crumbs
2 pats butter, cut into small
  pieces

Wash and trim the turnips. Cut off the greens and the roots. Scrub lightly to remove all the dirt from the outside. Place the turnips in a steamer, add enough water to steam the turnips, and bring the water to a hard boil over high heat. When the water starts to hard boil, let it boil for 5 minutes, then reduce the heat to a low boil and let the turnips steam for 10 more minutes. Then turn off the heat but leave the turnips in the steamer.

While the turnips are steaming in a large, heavy skillet over medium-high heat, add the ground round, pure pork sausage, and andouille and brown thoroughly, about 7 minutes. Add the onions, bell pepper, celery, garlic, and Cajun Seasoning Mix and sauté for 5 minutes, stirring constantly. Add the Tabasco® Sauce, garlic powder, and Worcestershire sauce then blend in well. Remove from the heat and set aside until ready to use.

Remove the turnips from the steamer and when they are cool enough to handle, scoop out the center and insides of the turnips, taking care to leave about $\frac{1}{2}$ inch of turnip all around the sides and bottom. You can use a spoon, but I find that a melon scoop works better and is more easily controlled. Put the pulp of the turnips in a mixing bowl and chop the pulp well when you are through. Add it to the meat skillet and return to the stove. Cook, stirring often, for 10 minutes over medium heat. Preheat the oven to 375 degrees. Add the rice, plain bread crumbs, green onion, and parsley and blend together well. Cook for 2 minutes, then remove from the heat.

When the mixture is cool enough to work with, fill the turnip shells with this stuffing, packing in as much of the mixture as possible. You will have more stuffing mixture than you need, but just put the remainder in a baking dish for use as a rice dressing side dish. You can also freeze the leftovers to use for stuffing a new batch of turnips at a later date. Sprinkle the tops of the turnips with the seasoned bread crumbs and dot with the butter pieces. Bake at 375 degrees for 30 minutes. The crust that forms on top will be a golden brown. Serve hot. Serves 8.

Lagniappe: This is really a great make-ahead dish. You can prepare the dish up to the baking and either freeze or refrigerate for later use. To heat, just defrost in the refrigerator and bake as directed. I generally like to make a big batch of stuffed turnips at one time, when the fresh, large young turnips hit the store. I keep some for a meal, then freeze a few batches for later use. It makes a great entrée or side dish.

If you can't find fresh large turnips, you can always make the dish without using large ones. Just make the dressing with whole turnips and place it into individual au gratin dishes and serve as a casserole. Having the turnip shells stuffed adds to the overall ambience and because of the eye appeal, the dish just tastes better that way.

You can also follow this same recipe and use shrimp or

crabmeat to make either Shrimp Stuffed Turnips or Lump Crabmeat Stuffed Turnips. Add $1^1/_2$ pounds of shrimp to the skillet when you add the meats or put in the lump crabmeat when you combine the rice and bread crumbs. Both are excellent. You will have a large amount of stuffing not used in the turnip shells, so I would recommend the leftovers be served as a casserole in individual au gratin dishes. Because the of the seafood addition, the dish can easily carry itself without the turnip shells.

MEATS AND MEAT DISHES

POULTRY

CHICKEN SAUCE PIQUANTE

1 large (5 to 6 lbs.) stewing hen, cut into 10 serving pieces
2 tsp. Cajun Seasoning Mix (see index)
1¼ cups peanut oil
1 cup flour
2 large onions, chopped
2 cups celery, chopped
2 med. bell peppers, chopped
¼ cup garlic, minced
1 can (16 oz.) whole tomatoes
2 cans (10 oz.) Ro-tel stewed tomatoes
2 cups mushroom, sliced
1 cup green onion bottoms, chopped
1½ qts. Chicken Stock (see index) or chicken broth
2 tsp. Tabasco® Sauce
1 tsp. salt
1 tsp. white pepper
½ tsp. cayenne pepper
1 cup green onion tops, minced
½ cup fresh parsley, minced
Cooked White Rice (see index)

Season each piece of chicken equally with the Cajun Seasoning Mix. Sauté the chicken in the peanut oil in a large, heavy saucepan over medium heat until all the pieces are nicely browned. Place the chicken on a warm platter for later use.

Add the flour to the pot and heat, stirring constantly, until you make a very dark reddish brown roux, almost the color of chocolate. Add the onions, celery, bell pepper, and garlic and then sauté for 5 minutes. Add the whole tomatoes, reserving the juice, and add the solid parts of the Ro-tel tomatoes, reserving their juice as well. Sauté the tomatoes, blending them into the roux and letting them break apart and dissolve, for about 5 more minutes.

Add the mushrooms and green onion bottoms, then sauté for 2 more minutes. Carefully add the Chicken Stock (it may splatter) and the juice from the tomatoes and stir into the roux mixture until a smooth sauce has developed. Add the Tabasco® Sauce, salt, and black, white, and cayenne pepper and blend in well. Reduce the heat to a low simmer and cook for 2 hours.

Add the chicken and make sure the pieces are covered by the liquid; cook for 3 hours, stirring occasionally, and cover the pot while cooking. The sauce should become very rich and tasty and the chicken very tender. Add the green onions and parsley and cook for 3 more minutes. Serve hot over cooked white rice. Serves 10.

Lagniappe: This is truly Cajun eating at its best! You can make this completely in advance and either refrigerate or freeze. The flavor seems to improve when it is allowed to sit in the refrigerator for a day. To reheat, just thaw in the refrigerator and bring the sauce back up to serving temperature over medium heat until it starts to boil, Then reduce to a low simmer. Cook for 25 minutes, then serve.

One excellent variation of this recipe that I really like is Rooster Sauce Piquante. Simply double the recipe and change the hen to a rooster (10 to 14 pounds) You will need to add $4^1/_2$ cups of stock, though, because you will cook the sauce for 5 to 6 hours at the low simmer after you add the rooster. This meat makes the dish much richer and gives it more depth. The rooster is just made for sauce piquante. After all that cooking, you will find the meat quite tasty and very tender. Of course, you can serve 18 to 20 people with this rooster version, or you will have plenty of delicious sauce piquante to freeze for later use.

Piquante means "hot" or "peppery," and to be real it must have quite a bite to it! If you can't take this much pepper, you can adjust the seasonings to your own taste. If you like it more peppered, just add 2 or 3 whole fresh cayenne peppers that you have minced to the dish with the onions. It will help to really "light up the dish!"

CHICKEN ETOUFFEE

1/2 cup cooking oil
2 tbsp. Cajun Seasoning Mix
   (see index)
1 whole (4 lbs.) fryer, cut
   into serving pieces
2 tbsp. flour, all-purpose
2 large onions, sliced
   lengthwise
1/4 cup carrots, finely chopped

1 med. bell pepper, chopped
1/2 cup celery, minced
3 cloves garlic, minced
1 tsp. Tabasco® Sauce
2 tsp. Worcestershire sauce
1/2 cup Chicken Stock (see
   index) or chicken broth
Cooked White Rice (see index)

Heat the oil in a large, heavy skillet that has a cover. Wash the chicken pieces and dry them well with paper towels. Coat the pieces of chicken evenly with the Cajun Seasoning Mix and fry them until they are brown on all sides. Remove the pieces as they brown to a warm plate. When all the chicken pieces are done, add the flour to the pot and cook, stirring constantly for 3 minutes. Return the chicken to the skillet and add all the remaining ingredients except the rice to the pot; reduce the heat to low and simmer for 1 hour, covered, or until the chicken is tender. Stir the dish about three times during the hour. Serve hot over cooked white rice. Serves 6.

Lagniappe: This dish can be prepared in advance and either frozen or refrigerated for later use. It will keep for up to 4 days in the refrigerator. To reheat, let the dish thaw in the refrigerator and cook it over low heat for 15 minutes, stirring occasionally. The chicken should be warm throughout. Étouffée means smothered, usually with lots of onions. So this is smothered chicken; it could also mean "choked," but serving choked chicken doesn't quite convey the true meaning!

CHICKEN FRICASSEE

1 large (4$\frac{1}{2}$ to 5 lbs.) stewing hen, cut into serving pieces
3 tsp. Cajun Seasoning Mix (see index)
$\frac{1}{2}$ cup bacon drippings
2 tbsp. butter, unsalted
2 tbsp. olive oil, extra virgin
$\frac{1}{2}$ cup flour, all-purpose
2 large onions, chopped
1 large bell pepper, chopped
1 cup celery, chopped
4 cloves garlic, minced
$\frac{1}{4}$ cup carrot, finely minced
1$\frac{1}{2}$ cups stewed tomatoes
1 lb. mushrooms, sliced
4 cups Chicken Stock (see index) or chicken broth
1 tsp. Tabasco® Sauce
1 tbsp. Worcestershire sauce
1 cup dry red wine
2 whole bay leaves
$\frac{2}{3}$ cup green onion tops, minced
$\frac{1}{4}$ cup parsley
Cooked white long-grain rice (see index)

Wash the chicken with tap water and dry it with paper towels. Season the chicken pieces evenly with the Cajun Seasoning Mix. In a heavy metal saucepot, melt the bacon drippings and butter over medium-high heat. When the oils are hot, brown the chicken pieces. Remove the chicken to a warm platter when they are browned. Add the olive oil and flour and cook over medium heat until the flour is a dark brown, almost the color of fudge or dark chocolate.

Stir constantly with a flexible wire whisk, making sure that none of the flour sticks. When the dark brown color is reached, add the onions, bell pepper, celery, garlic, and carrots to the roux and cook, stirring constantly for 5 minutes. Add the stewed tomatoes and sauté them for 2 more minutes. Add the mushrooms and stir them into the roux. Add the Chicken Stock, Tabasco® Sauce, Worcestershire sauce, red wine, and bay leaves, then mix well until a nice sauce has formed. Add the chicken pieces to the pot and reduce the heat to a low simmer. Cook for $2^1/_2$ to 3 hours or until the chicken is tender. Just before serving add the green onions and parsley and cook for 3 more minutes. Serve hot over cooked white rice. Serves 6 to 8.

Lagniappe: Fricassée is basically a stew. The technique used is braising, or cooking the meat slowly in a simmering liquid. It helps to tenderize the meat and intensifies the flavor of the sauce (gravy) as the meat cooks. While this is not difficult, it does take time. My grandmother always used to say, *"Cher, cook with your heart and soul, and mais, dat takes lots of time and love, cher!"*

When we cook for others, it doesn't matter that we put ourselves out. What matters is creating a feast for your family and friends. This recipe puts it all in the pot. You can make this dish completely in advance and refrigerate for up to 4 days before serving or you can freeze the dish for later use. Since it has its own liquid to cook in, just heat the dish over a low, simmering heat until the chicken is hot. Then serve almost always over cooked white rice.

CHICKEN JAMBALAYA

2 med. (2 lbs. ea.) fryers
$^1/_4$ cup peanut oil
3 tsp. Cajun Seasoning Mix
  (see index)
1 cup baked ham, cut into
  cubes
1 lb. pure pork sausage, sliced
  into $^1/_2$-inch circles
2 large onions, chopped
2 med. bell peppers, chopped
$1^1/_2$ cups celery, chopped
4 cloves garlic, minced
1 can ($14^1/_2$ oz.) stewed
  tomatoes

1 tbsp. Dark Brown Roux
  (see index)
5 cups Chicken Stock (see
  index) or chicken broth
$^1/_2$ cup dry white wine
1 tsp. salt
1 tsp. cayenne pepper
1 tsp. onion powder
1 tsp. garlic powder
1 tsp. Tabasco® Sauce
$2^1/_2$ cups raw long-grain rice
1 whole bay leaf
$^3/_4$ cup green onions, minced
$^1/_2$ cup fresh parsley, minced

Wash the fryer well with tap water, then cut it into serving pieces and pat the chicken dry with dry paper towels. Season the chicken with the Cajun Seasoning Mix. Add the peanut oil to a large, heavy skillet that has a lid, and let the oil get hot and start to smoke over medium-high heat. Fry the chicken pieces until they are well browned, then remove to a warm platter for later use. Add the ham and sausage to the skillet and sauté for 5 minutes, stirring constantly.

Remove the meat to a plate and set aside. Sauté the onions, bell pepper, celery, and garlic for 5 minutes over medium heat in the oil left in the skillet. While the vegetables are sautéing, drain the tomatoes and reserve the liquid. Add the tomatoes and Dark Brown Roux to the skillet and sauté for 2 minutes. Add the chicken, ham, and sausage back to the skillet and add the Chicken Stock and liquid from the tomatoes as well as the white wine. Let the dish cook over low heat, covered, for 15 minutes.

Add the remaining ingredients except for the green onions and parsley and bring the liquid to a boil. Once it is boiling, stir well, cover, and reduce the heat to low and cook, covered, for 30 minutes over very low heat. The water should all be absorbed by the rice or evaporated, and the rice should be tender. Remove the cover and add the green onions and parsley, then stir them into the dish until well blended. Cover and let the jambalaya cook over very low heat for 3 minutes, then serve hot. Serves 6 to 8.

Lagniappe: Jambalaya was originally a "clean out the ice box" dish. It is one of the dishes that has made Louisiana Cajun food famous. It got its name from two words: the French word for ham, "jambon," and the African word for rice, "yaya." So it was basically ham and rice. But the Cajuns decided to take this dish to new heights. Old recipes all had ham, but today we make jambalaya with any meat we happen to have.

To be honest, we actually go out and buy the assortment of meats we put in our jambalayas. You can make a great Pork Jambalaya by using the recipe above and substituting pork chops for the chicken and leaving the rest of the recipe as is. Just season the chops with the seasoning mix and brown as you would the chicken. Then follow the recipe as above.

Another way to go is to use fresh Louisiana seafood and make a Shrimp and Oyster Jambalaya. Use 1 quart of oysters and 2 pounds of shrimp instead of the chicken. Change the peanut oil to butter and season the shrimp with 2 teaspoons of the seasoning mix, reserving the other teaspoon to season the oysters. Put the oysters into a mixing bowl, season with the teaspoon of Cajun Seasoning Mix, and let them sit. Sauté the shrimp in the butter and remove to a warm platter as you did the chicken. Proceed with the recipe as above, cooking the shrimp with the ham and sausage for 15 minutes. When you add the rice, add the oysters that you have in the bowl as well and follow the recipe exactly as above.

This will give you a dramatically different jambalaya, but one that you'll savor for a long time. Be creative, just like the old Cajun cooks. Use the meats that you have in your "ice box" and enjoy the true Cajun creative spirit of the dish.

POULTRY

PAN-FRIED CHICKEN

1 large (3½ to 4 lbs.) fryer, cut into serving pieces
2 tsp. Cajun Seasoning Mix (see index)
1 cup prepared mustard
1 tbsp. Tabasco® Sauce
2 large eggs, well beaten
½ cup heavy whipping cream
1 tsp. Tabasco® Sauce
1 tbsp. fresh parsley, very finely minced
2 tsp. Worcestershire sauce
1 tsp. salt
1 tsp. cayenne pepper
1 tsp. black pepper, freshly ground
1½ tbsp. cornstarch
2 cups flour
½ cup bacon drippings
1 cup peanut oil

Wash the chicken pieces with tap water, rinsing them well. Pat them dry with dry paper towels, then season the pieces equally with the Cajun Seasoning Mix. In a large mixing bowl, add the mustard and Tabasco® Sauce and mix together well. Add the seasoned chicken pieces and coat each of the pieces well with the mustard. Cover the bowl with plastic wrap and refrigerate for at least 2 hours up to 24. When you are ready to cook, remove the chicken and shake off any excess mustard.

In a large mixing bowl add the eggs, whipping cream, the remaining Tabasco® Sauce, parsley, and Worcestershire sauce; combine by beating with the whisk. Add the chicken and let the pieces soak in the egg mixture. In another large mixing bowl combine the salt, cayenne and black pepper, cornstarch, and flour; mix well to make sure the ingredients have combined. Take each piece of chicken out of the egg mixture and dip them into the flour. Then place them on a large platter.

Heat the bacon drippings and peanut oil in a large, heavy metal skillet over medium heat. When the oil is hot, dip the chicken piece by piece back into the egg mixture, then dredge it back in the flour. Add the pieces to the skillet one at a time, using the largest pieces first, until all are in the skillet. Cook until all sides of the chicken pieces are a beautiful dark brown, about 20 to 25 minutes, turning often to make sure none of the chicken burns. Remove the chicken pieces from the skillet and let them drain on layers of dry paper towels. Serve at once. Serves 6.

Lagniappe: When Cajuns fried chicken, they pan fried rather than deep fried the chicken pieces. This makes for a darker outer color but a more intensely flavored fried chicken. The use of bacon drippings also greatly adds flavor to the chicken. Pan-fried chicken allows the chicken to slowly cook and intensify the flavor of the "crust" and the chicken.

You can use this same recipe to make Pan-Fried Quail by substituting 4 whole quail, cut in half, lengthwise, for the chicken in the recipe. If you like rabbit, use this same recipe and substitute a large rabbit or 2 smaller ones for the chicken. Cut the rabbit into serving pieces and follow the recipe to make Pan-Fried Rabbit. This is an easy recipe to follow and gets rave reviews.

POULTRY

BAKED CHICKEN

1 large (4 to 4$\frac{1}{2}$ lbs.) fryer
1 tbsp. Cajun Seasoning Mix
  (see index)
2 med. turnips, fresh , tender,
  young, and cut in half
6 med. carrots, cleaned and
  cut in half
4 stalks celery, cleaned and
  cut in thirds
1 small Granny Smith apple,
  cored, seeded, and cut in
  half

12 med. new potatoes, cleaned
12 whole mushrooms,
  trimmed, with grit removed
1 large bell pepper, julienned
1 large onion, cut in slices,
  lengthwise
1 tsp. Tabasco® Sauce
1 tbsp. Worcestershire sauce
2 tbsp. Dark Brown Roux
  (see index)
1 cup dry white wine

Preheat the oven to 450 degrees. Wash the chicken well
and cut off any excess fat. Pat the chicken dry with the
paper towels. Season well with the seasoning mix, both
inside the cavity and outside the chicken. Fill the chicken's
cavity with the turnips, 1 carrot, 1 stalk of celery, and the
apple. Place the chicken in a large baking dish and bake at
450 degrees for 30 minutes. The chicken should be nicely
browned. Remove from the oven and lower the heat to
350 degrees. Take the chicken out of the baking dish and
add the remaining ingredients to the dish. Stir to help the
roux dissolve in the liquid. Return the chicken to the dish,
placing it on top of the vegetables. Then cover, return to
the oven, and bake for 1 hour.

Remove the dish from the oven, increase the heat to
400 degrees, and stir the vegetables at the bottom of the
dish well. Then return the chicken to the oven and bake
for 30 more minutes at 400 degrees. The chicken should
be a golden brown and tender, and the vegetables
cooked. Remove the chicken from the dish and place in

the center of a large serving platter. Spoon the vegetables on the platter surrounding the chicken and serve at once. Serves 6.

Lagniappe: This is an excellent simple dish that offers great contrasts. You not only have your meat, but also a nice array of fresh vegetables. This is not a dish that you would want to make in advance, because the vegetables will really be at their peak if eaten right after cooking. You can do all the preparation for the dish in advance, then all you have to do is put it together and bake. You can use this same recipe to make Baked Duck. Use a 4$\frac{1}{2}$- to 5-pound duck and follow the recipe. Do everything exactly as shown except you should increase the first baking time from 30 minutes to 45 minutes and the second from 1 hour to 1$\frac{1}{2}$ hours. Everything else remains the exactly the same.

Be sure not to use wild ducks with this recipe. It is designed for store-bought domestic ducklings. You will have to skim off some of the grease that will be present, since the ducklings have a significantly greater amount of fat.

PAN-ROASTED WILD DUCK

3 whole (1¹/₂ to 2 lbs. ea.) wild ducks
3 tsp. Cajun Seasoning Mix (see index)
1 large onion, cut into thirds
1 large green apple, seeds removed and cut into thirds
1 large tender turnip, washed, trimmed, and cut into thirds
1 large carrot, cleaned and cut into thirds
1 large stalk celery, cleaned and cut into thirds
3 strips bacon
3 tbsp. peanut oil
1 large onion, chopped
1 large bell pepper, julienned
3 cloves garlic, minced
2 tbsp. Dark Brown Roux (see index)
¹/₂ cup dry white wine
1 tsp. Tabasco® Sauce
1 cup Chicken Stock (see index) or chicken broth
Cooked White Rice (see index)

Wash the ducks and pat them dry with dry paper towels. Use 1 of the teaspoons of seasoning mix and season the inside of the duck cavities. Arrange the onion, apple, turnip, carrot, celery, and bacon inside the duck cavities, then truss the ducks closed with kitchen string.

Heat the peanut oil in a heavy metal skillet that has a cover and is large enough to hold the three ducks. While the oil is heating, season the outside of the ducks with the remaining seasoning. Sauté the ducks until they are nicely browned on all sides, about 5 minutes. Remove the ducks to a warm platter for later use.

Add the onions, garlic, and bell pepper and sauté in the remaining oil for 3 minutes. Then add the Dark Brown Roux and blend in well. Add the wine, Tabasco® Sauce, and Chicken Stock and blend together well. Return the ducks to the skillet. Cover and cook for 1¹/₂ hours over medium-low heat. When the time is up, check the ducks for tenderness. The sauce should be brown and the ducks tender. If not, cover and cook for 15 more minutes. Cooking time will vary depending on the size and type of duck, but it should not vary more than the 15 minutes. Serve at once with cooked white rice. Serves 6.

Lagniappe: This dish is so great right from the pot, but you can refrigerate or freeze for later use after completely cooking. To reheat, just thaw in the refrigerator and heat in a covered pan for about 15 minutes over medium heat. You can always add a small amount of water if the gravy gets too thick. To serve, place the ducks, cut in half, on a platter surrounded by the vegetables that cooked in the duck cavities and covered with the nice gravy that has been created from the juices, sautéed vegetables, and roux. Set the cooked white rice in a bowl on the side. What a nice presentation!

VEGETABLES

BEANS AND RICE

1 lb. dried red beans, navy
   beans, or Great Northern
   white beans
Water to cover and soak
3 tbsp. butter, unsalted
1 med. onion, chopped
1 med. bell pepper, chopped
$^1/_2$ cup celery, minced
3 cloves garlic, minced
1 lb. ham, cut into $^1/_2$-inch
   blocks, or smoked sausage
   or andouille, cut into
   $^1/_2$-inch pieces

1 cup green onions, chopped
$^1/_2$ cup parsley, minced
1 tsp. salt
1 tsp. black pepper
1 tsp. cayenne pepper
$^1/_2$ tsp. thyme
2 whole bay leaves
2 tsp. Tabasco® Sauce
1 tbsp. Worcestershire sauce
Chicken Stock (see index) or
   broth to cover
Cooked White Rice (see index)

Put the beans in a large pot and cover them with water. Cover and let the beans soak overnight. When you are ready to cook, use a large, heavy saucepan over medium-high heat. Add the butter and when it is melted, add the onion, bell pepper, celery, and garlic. Sauté for 7 minutes, stirring constantly. Add the ham or sausage and the remaining ingredients, up to the Chicken Stock. Mix together well and cook for 2 minutes, stirring often. Add the chicken stock to cover the beans completely, reduce the heat to simmer, and cook until the beans are tender, about $2^1/_2$ to 3 hours. Serve hot over cooked white rice. Serves 8.

Lagniappe: Bean dishes made their way with the Cajuns from their homeland in Acadie (Nova Scotia). The beans, of course, made their way to Canada from France. This dish is deeply rooted in the history of the Acadian people and thus the Cajuns. Depending on the area the Cajuns settled, the favorite bean changed from small white navy beans (the favorite of the Cajuns from St. Martinsville, my ancestors) to large white beans and dark red kidney beans (the favorite of the Cajuns near New Orleans).

The dish varies with the bean used and with the meats chosen to season the dish. The meat is usually some form of smoked pork or smoked pork sausage. The choice is pretty much left to you. This dish is actually better if made the day before you serve it and then refrigerated, to be used the next day. The flavors tend to intensify when the beans are allowed to refrigerate for at least 24 hours.

I do not like to freeze the dish, because the beans have already broken apart quite a bit in the cooking process and freezing them tends to completely break the beans apart. You are left with a tasty dish but one that tends to be less appealing to the eye. You can always add additional meat to the dish or serve an additional meat with the meal if you like.

SMOTHERED CABBAGE

3 tbsp. bacon fat	1 tsp. black pepper, fresh
1 large onion, chopped	ground
1 head large cabbage	1 tsp. Tabasco® Sauce
1½ cups water	1 tbsp. sugar
1 tsp. salt	1 strip bacon, chopped

Melt the bacon fat over medium heat in a large, heavy skillet that has a cover. Add the onion and sauté until it is limp, about 5 minutes at medium-high heat. Add the cabbage and sauté it for 5 minutes over medium heat. Add the remaining ingredients, mix well, and cover. Reduce the heat to low and simmer until the cabbage is done, about 25 minutes. Serve hot. Serves 6 to 8.

Lagniappe: Although this dish is best served right after cooking, you can make it in advance and either refrigerate or freeze it. To reheat, thaw in the refrigerator if frozen and cook in a covered skillet until the cabbage is hot. For variety you can add ham hocks to the cabbage instead of bacon. Be sure your skillet is large enough to hold the ham hocks and cabbage. If you use ham hocks, add the ham hocks before you add the onion. Cook the hocks, covered, for about 20 minutes, at medium heat, shaking the skillet, but not removing the cover, every few minutes. Then remove the hocks and follow the directions above. Add the hocks back when you add the bacon and cook as above. Either way, smothered cabbage is a crowd pleaser.

VEGETABLES

GLAZED CARROTS

1 bunch fresh young carrots,
   cleaned and trimmed
Water to cover
1 tsp. salt
1 tsp. sugar
3 tbsp. butter, unsalted
3 tbsp. light brown sugar

2 tbsp. dark brown sugar
$^1/_2$ tsp. ginger
$^1/_4$ tsp. nutmeg
$^1/_2$ tsp. Tabasco® Sauce
1 tbsp. fresh lemon juice
$^1/_2$ tsp. salt

Scrape the outside layer off the carrots gently with a knife and cut the carrots diagonally into 1-inch pieces. In a saucepan that has a lid, add the carrots and cover with water. Add the teaspoon of salt and sugar and bring the water to a boil over medium-high heat, covered, for about 7 minutes or until the carrots are tender. Remove from the heat and drain well.

In a heavy skillet over medium-high heat, melt the butter. Add the carrots and sauté them for 2 minutes, making sure all are coated with the butter. Add the brown sugars, ginger, nutmeg, and Tabasco® Sauce. Stir constantly until the sugar is melted and the carrots are coated with the light glaze, about 4 minutes. Add the lemon juice and remaining salt and blend in well. Serve hot at once. Serves 4 to 6.

Lagniappe: For the peak flavor, serve the dish soon after cooking. However, you can make it in advance and freeze or refrigerate. To use, just thaw in the refrigerator and warm in the microwave or in a skillet with a cover. Cook over low heat until the carrots are warm. This is the carrot dish that you serve to get kids to eat carrots. You get all the goodness of carrots, and the kids get a dish that is sweet and good to eat. When the fresh young carrots are plentiful is the best time to make this dish. Tender young carrots are really super in this dish.

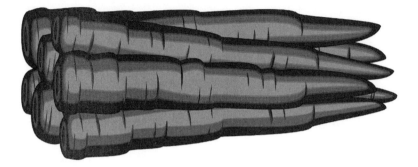

CAULIFLOWER AU GRATIN

1 head large cauliflower
Water to steam
$^1/_4$ cup butter, unsalted
3 tbsp. flour, all-purpose
1 can (13 oz.) evaporated milk
$^1/_4$ cup milk
4 oz. American cheese, grated
1 tsp. Tabasco® Sauce
$^1/_2$ tsp. onion powder

$^1/_2$ tsp. black pepper, fresh
  ground
$^1/_2$ tsp. salt
3 large eggs, yolks only
Butter to grease the baking
  dish
Paprika to dust the top of the
  dish

Clean and wash the cauliflower. Cut off the green leaves and remove the center core. Place the cauliflower in a steamer with enough water to bring up a good bit of steam. Steam the head for 5 minutes over high heat, then turn off the heat and let the head stand in the steamer until you are ready to use.

Preheat the oven to 350 degrees. In a large saucepan over medium heat, melt the butter. Add the flour and blend it in well. Cook the flour for 3 minutes over medium heat, stirring constantly. Remove from the heat and add the evaporated milk and regular milk; blend it in well, then return it to the heat. Cook, stirring constantly, until the sauce thickens and gets smooth. Add the cheese, Tabasco® Sauce, onion powder, black pepper, and salt. Reduce the heat to low and cook until all the cheese has melted and the sauce is smooth.

In a medium mixing bowl, add the egg yolks and beat them with a wire whisk until they are smooth and have added about one-third to their volume. Spoon some of the hot mixture into the bowl and mix it in with the wire whisk until it is smooth again. Continue the same process until you have doubled the amount of liquid in the mixing bowl, then slowly pour the egg mixture back into the saucepan.

Stir the two mixtures together until the cheese sauce is quite smooth. Remove the pan from the heat. Grease a 12x12 baking dish with the butter for greasing and arrange the cauliflower in the dish. Pour the cheese sauce over the flowerets and sprinkle lightly with the paprika. Bake in the 350-degree oven for 30 minutes. The sauce should be bubbling and the top a golden brown. Serve hot. Serves 6 to 8.

Lagniappe: If a steamer is not available, you can either microwave the cauliflower with a little water in the bottom of the dish or you can boil it in a large sauce pot that has a lid. Boiling is the last resort, because it removes so much of the natural vitamins that you'll get in either the steamer or microwave.

This dish may be made in advance and put into the refrigerator or freezer for later use. Just thaw in the refrigerator and bake at 300 degrees until the dish is hot, about 10 minutes, or you can put it in the microwave until it is warm. This was a dish that we were only able to have in the late fall and winter in the past, because that's the only time we could get fresh cauliflower. Today, we get it year round. We kind of take for granted the many wonderful vegetables that are now available throughout the year.

VEGETABLES

CUSHAW

1 med. cushaw (about 6
   to 8 lbs.)
3 cups water
¹/₂ stick butter
2 cups sugar
¹/₂ cup brown sugar

1 tsp. cinnamon
1 tsp. nutmeg
¹/₂ tsp. cloves
¹/₂ tsp. allspice
¹/₂ tsp. round ginger
1 tbsp. vanilla extract

Cut the cushaw in half and remove all the seeds and strings around the seeds. Peel it and cut it into 1-inch cubes. Put into a large, heavy pot that has a cover, add the water and butter, and bring to a hard boil. Once the water starts to hard boil, wait 2 minutes, then reduce the heat to a simmer and cover. Let the cushaw cook for about 40 minutes, covered, stirring a few times to prevent sticking and to make sure that it cooks evenly. Remove the cover and add the remaining ingredients and cook until most of the liquid has evaporated, stirring often during the cooking process. After most of the liquid has evaporated, about 20 to 30 minutes, the cushaw should be smooth and nicely browned and ready to serve. Serve hot. Serves 10 to 12.

Lagniappe: This is a wonderful Cajun pumpkin dish. The cushaw is the white-and-green striped, crook-necked pumpkin you see for sale on roadside stands all over the state during pumpkin season. My grandfather used to raise hundreds to sell to stores in the area every fall. More often they are sold at small stands. When you find them in the store, they usually sell by the pound, which is not the way to buy them, since they are quite large and lose so much of their weight in the cooking process. We used to keep the cushaw in a cool, dry place so they would last most of the winter. This is a sweet vegetable dish that complements most meals.

MAQUE CHOUX (SMOTHERED CORN)

12 ears sweet fresh corn
1 large onion, chopped
1 med. bell pepper, finely
  diced
2 large tomatoes, skinned and
  chopped
2 cloves garlic, minced

1 tbsp. sugar
1 tsp. Tabasco® Sauce
1 tsp. salt
1 tsp. black pepper, freshly
  ground
3 tbsp. cooking oil
1 tbsp. butter, unsalted

Cut the corn off each cob by standing the ear on one end in a large bowl and scraping the kernels off from the middle to the bottom with a downward motion all around the ear. Then repeat the process from the other end. Make sure you scrape all of the milk from the cob. Repeat the process until all 12 ears are cut.

Mix the corn, onion, bell pepper, tomatoes, and garlic. Add the sugar, Tabasco® Sauce, salt, and black pepper; blend in well. In a large heavy skillet that has a cover, add the oil and heat it over medium-high heat. When the oil is hot, add the butter, then add the corn mixture. Cook for 10 minutes, stirring constantly to keep the dish from sticking. Reduce the heat to low and simmer, covered, for about 20 minutes or until the corn is tender. Serve hot. Serves 6 to 8.

Lagniappe: I guess this is my favorite vegetable of all time. It is pronounced "mock shoe" and may be made in advance, refrigerated, or even frozen for later use. After thawing, reheat in a covered skillet over low heat until the dish is warm, about 7 minutes. I have to say, Maque Choux is good hot or cold. It is one of the premier Cajun specialties. You can serve it as a vegetable with almost any meal. Some even like to add meat such as chicken or pork and serve it as a one-dish meal. When the corn is fresh, this is company eating, but it's delicious enough to eat anytime.

EGGPLANT DEBORAH

2 large eggplants, 1 peeled, the other with the peeling on, both cut into fourths
Water to cover the eggplant
1 tsp. salt
5 strips bacon, chopped
1 stick butter, unsalted
1 large onion, chopped
1 large bell pepper, chopped
2 stalks celery, diced
3 cloves garlic, minced
1 tsp. Tabasco® Sauce
$1/2$ tsp. garlic powder
$1/2$ tsp. onion powder
$1/2$ tsp. sweet basil
1 tbsp. lemon juice, freshly squeezed
3 cups Ritz cracker crumbs
$1/2$ tsp. salt
1 tsp. black pepper, freshly ground
$1/4$ cup plain bread crumbs
2 pats butter, cut into pieces

Preheat the oven to 350 degrees. Place the eggplant in a large saucepan and cover with water. Add the 1 teaspoon of salt and bring the water to a boil over high heat. When the water comes to a hard boil, let it boil for 2 minutes, then turn off the heat. Let the eggplant sit in the water until you are ready to use it.

In another large heavy skillet, sauté the bacon until it is brown and crisp, but do not burn it. Melt the butter in the skillet with the bacon, then add the onion, bell pepper, celery, and garlic. Sauté the vegetables for 5 minutes over medium-high heat, stirring constantly. The onions should be clear. Remove the eggplant from the water with a slotted spoon; reserve the water for possible use. Place the eggplant in the skillet and sauté it for 5 minutes. Season with the Tabasco® Sauce, garlic powder, onion powder, sweet basil, and lemon juice.

Blend in the cracker crumbs, salt, and black pepper. Add liquid from the eggplant stock pot as is needed to keep the mixture from being too dry, usually about $^1/_2$ to 1 cup. Pour the eggplant mixture into a large, deep casserole dish (12x18) and sprinkle lightly with the bread crumbs. Dot the top with the butter pieces and bake at 350 degrees for 30 minutes. The top should be nicely browned. Serve hot. Serves 8 to 10.

Lagniappe: Eggplant at its best! This is a great dish by itself and a wonderful base for other dishes. Add ham, chicken, shrimp, oysters, or crabmeat to turn it into a very special main dish. You can make it in advance and refrigerate or freeze, even if you add meat or seafood to it. You can also keep the eggplant shells and stuff this recipe back into the shells and bake. It makes a wonderful Stuffed Eggplant. Be creative and add the ingredients you like to the eggplant and turn a great meal into an exceptional one.

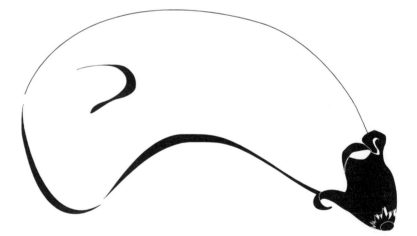

STUFFED MIRLITON

6 whole mirlitons (vegetable
  pear or Chayote squash)
Water to steam
3 strips bacon, chopped
6 tbsp. butter, unsalted
1 large onion, chopped
1 med. red bell pepper, diced
2 stalks celery, minced
3 cloves garlic, minced
1$^1/_2$ cups baked ham, diced
1 lb. shrimp, coarsely chopped

1 cup Ritz cracker crumbs
1 tsp. Tabasco® Sauce
1 tbsp. Worcestershire sauce
1$^1/_2$ tsp. Cajun Seasoning Mix
  (see index)
1 tbsp. lemon juice, freshly
  squeezed
$^1/_2$ cup seasoned bread crumbs
3 pats butter, cut into small
  pieces

Steam the mirlitons by bringing the water in a steamer to a boil. When the water has begun to boil, steam for 7 minutes, then turn off the heat. Let the mirlitons stay in the steamer until you are ready for them. In a large, heavy skillet over medium-high heat, fry the bacon pieces until they are browned and crisp. Add the 6 tablespoons of butter and remove from the heat and and set aside. Remove the mirlitons from the steamer and cut each of them in half. Remove the large seed and discard. Scoop out the center of the mirliton with a teaspoon or melon ball scoop, taking care not to tear through the outer shell of the vegetable, and place in a large bowl.

When all the inside of the mirliton is removed into the bowl, set the shells aside for later use in stuffing. Use a potato masher or a large slotted spoon to mash the pulp that you removed from the mirliton. Return the skillet containing the butter and bacon to a medium-high heat and add the mirliton pulp as well as the onion, bell pepper, celery, and garlic. Sauté for 10 minutes, stirring often to prevent sticking.

Preheat the oven to 350 degrees. Add the ham and shrimp and sauté for 7 more minutes, stirring constantly. Add the cracker crumbs to the vegetable and blend in well. Add the Tabasco® Sauce, Worcestershire, Cajun Seasoning Mix, and lemon juice; mix in well. Stuff each of the mirliton shells that have been set aside, making sure you stuff each equally. Sprinkle the bread crumbs over the stuffing and dot with the butter pieces. Bake at 350 degrees for 35 to 40 minutes or until well browned. Serve hot. Serves 12 as a side dish or vegetable.

Lagniappe: Although this is a vegetable, it can be used as a main dish. Just serve two per person instead of one. You should have no problem finding mirlitons around the country, mainly because this South American squash has become a mainstay of the spreading Latino population. It used to be available on a seasonal basis in Louisiana but is now available year round. This is an exceptional complement to any meal. The stuffing and the nice green shell make for a great contrast. You can also be very creative in adding to the stuffing.

You can substitute smoked sausage for the ham and crabmeat or oysters for the shrimp. Or you can make it only with meat or only with seafood. It is also quite wonderful without any meat or seafood. The combinations are limited only by your imagination. You can prepare in advance and refrigerate or freeze for later use. It holds up very well. This is truly an exceptional Cajun dish. The Cajuns who returned home from exile in South America in the mid-1700s brought this staple back with them, and it has been enjoyed since. It's truly a well-traveled Cajun dish.

MUSTARD GREENS

2 bunches mustard greens
  (about 2 lbs.)
Water to cover
$^1/_4$ lb. salt pork, cut into
  1-inch pieces

1 tsp. salt
1 tsp. Tabasco® Sauce
1 tsp. sugar
$^1/_2$ tsp. black pepper
$^1/_2$ cup onions, finely chopped

Soak the greens in water, for 2 minutes, then clean each by cutting off any thick stems or bad pieces. Place the greens in a large, heavy pot and add enough water to cover. Add the remaining ingredients and bring the mixture to a boil over high heat. When it begins to boil, let it cook at high heat for 4 minutes, then reduce the heat to a low simmer, covered, for about 25 minutes or until the greens are tender.

Remove the greens from the pot to a large bowl and bring the pot liquor to a hard boil until the liquid is reduced by two-thirds. Then return the greens to the pot and let them simmer for about 3 minutes until they are well reheated. Pour them into a serving dish and serve at once. Serves 6 to 8.

Lagniappe: This is mustard greens at their best. You can reduce the step a bit by not covering the greens and just letting the water evaporate, but you do lose some of the intense flavor that comes from just reducing the water after the cooking process is complete. I do it both ways, depending on the time I have. Generally, I do it right when I'm cooking for company and the other way when I'm just cooking for family. Mustard greens are an acquired taste, but look out. Once acquired, the taste becomes addictive. It's a good thing they are so easy to grow and inexpensive to buy.

SMOTHERED OKRA AND TOMATOES

3 lbs. fresh okra
$1/2$ cup cooking oil
1 large onion, chopped
1 med. bell pepper, chopped
2 stalks celery, minced
4 cloves garlic, minced

4 large ripe tomatoes, skin
  removed and diced
$1^1/2$ tsp. Cajun Seasoning Mix
  (see index)
1 tsp. Tabasco® Sauce

Cut the okra into 1-inch circles. Make sure to select tender young okra that is not too hard. The knife should be able to cut through the okra with almost no effort. In a large, heavy sauce pan that has a lid, add the oil and let it get hot over medium-high heat. When the oil is hot, add the okra and sauté the okra, onions, bell pepper, celery, and garlic for 15 minutes, stirring often. Cover and reduce the heat to low and let the okra and vegetables cook for 15 more minutes, stirring a few times. The slime should be gone. Add the tomatoes, Cajun Seasoning Mix, and Tabasco® Sauce; stir in well and cover. Continue to cook covered for about 30 more minutes or until the okra is tender, stirring occasionally. Serve hot. Serves 8.

Lagniappe: This is the traditional way to cook okra. If you'd like a less involved way, just preheat the oven to 375 degrees. Combine all the ingredients in a heavy pot that has a tight lid and put in the oven, covered, for 30 minutes. Remove and stir thoroughly, cover, and return to the oven for 30 more minutes—and the dish is done.

    I have to tell you, this is the method I use now! The outcome tastes the same, and the dish looks nicer to me since the okra still has shape and looks like cut okra rather than the broken-apart look you get from the constant stirring. I especially like the oven method when I'm pressed for time and when I'm adding the smothered okra to a gumbo. It makes the whole process easier.

Okra is a vegetable that the Cajuns got from the local Africans in the 1700s. The name "gumbo" comes from okra, which was the African word for the vegetable.

SQUASH CASSEROLE

2 lbs. tender yellow squash, cleaned and trimmed
Water to steam
4 strips bacon, chopped
$^1/_2$ stick butter, unsalted
$^1/_4$ cup olive oil
1 large onion, chopped
1 med. bell pepper, chopped
$^1/_2$ cup celery, diced
3 cloves garlic, minced

1 tsp. Tabasco® Sauce
1 tbsp. Worcestershire sauce
$^1/_2$ tsp. onion powder
$1^1/_2$ tsp. Cajun Seasoning Mix (see index)
$^1/_2$ cup fresh parsley, minced
2 cups Ritz cracker crumbs
$^1/_4$ cup bread seasoned bread crumbs
2 pats butter, cut into pieces

Preheat the oven to 350 degrees. Put the squash into a steamer and bring the water to a boil over high heat in the steamer. Once the water starts to boil, steam for 3 minutes, then turn the heat off, but leave the squash in the steamer.

In a large, heavy skillet, sauté the bacon until it is brown and crisp over medium high heat, stirring often. Add the butter and olive oil and let the butter melt. When the butter is melted, add the onions, bell pepper, celery, and garlic and sauté, stirring constantly for 5 minutes over medium-high heat.

While the vegetables are sautéing, remove the squash from the steamer and cut them into $^1/_2$-inch circles. Put the sliced squash into the sautéed vegetables and sauté for 5 more minutes. Add the remaining ingredients except for the bread crumbs and butter pats, and blend in well. Pour the squash into a lightly buttered casserole dish and sprinkle the top with the seasoned bread crumbs. Dot the top, evenly, with the butter pieces and bake at 350 degrees for 35 to 40 minutes. Serve hot. Serves 8.

Lagniappe: Although this recipe is best when it is first cooked, it does refrigerate and freeze well. Freeze in an ovenproof dish to save time when reheating to serve later. In the past, yellow squash was available only in the summer, thus the name Summer Squash. But today it is available year round. This dish is great no matter what time of the year you serve it. It makes a nice addition to most meals. The color is nice—yellow and browns from the baking. It is also a great way to serve yellow squash since it is so easy to cook. It's great as a side dish with any meal or as a nice salad.

WHITE RICE

2 cups raw rice	1 tsp. salt
2 cups water	

Wash the rice thoroughly to remove any items that need to be cleaned away. Rinse until the water is clear. Drain and put the rice into a heavy saucepot that is at least 6 cups in size and has a cover. Add the water and salt. Put on medium-high heat and bring to a boil. When the rice starts to boil, stir it well and cover. Reduce the heat to low and cook for 15 to 20 minutes or until all the water has evaporated. The rice should be tender and hot. Serves 6 to 8.

Lagniappe: You almost have to know how to cook rice to be a Cajun. Rice is such a Cajun staple. We eat rice at almost every meal, sometimes even at breakfast. It is served with gravies, stews, gumbos, sauce piquantes, étouffées, fricassées, and a variety of beans. We also make a number of dressings with it. It would be hard to eat in Cajun country without finding a rice dish or two.

VEGETABLES

DIRTY RICE (RICE DRESSING)

$^1/_2$ lb. ground pork
$^1/_2$ lb. ground beef
1 lb. chicken livers,
2 tbsp. flour, all-purpose
1 large onion, chopped
1 large bell pepper, finely diced
1 cup celery, minced
3 cloves garlic, minced

2 cups White Rice (see index)
1$^1/_2$ tsp. Cajun Seasoning Mix
  (see index)
1 tsp. Tabasco® Sauce
1 tsp. Worcestershire Sauce
1 cup green onions, minced
$^1/_2$ cup parsley, finely minced

In a large, heavy skillet over medium-high heat, add the ground pork and beef and sauté until the meat is nicely browned, about 10 minutes. Add the chicken livers, reduce the heat to medium, and sauté, stirring often, for 10 more minutes; then add the flour. Cook for 7 minutes, stirring constantly to keep the flour from sticking. The livers should break apart and the ground meats should be well blended into small pieces. Add the onion, bell pepper, celery, and garlic and sauté for 5 more minutes, stirring constantly. Turn the heat to low, cover, and let the mixture simmer for 15 minutes. Add the remaining ingredients and mix thoroughly. Serve hot. Serves 8 to 10.

Lagniappe: This is the premier Cajun rice dish. You aren't really Cajun if you don't eat Dirty Rice! The name comes from the way the rice looks because of the broken chicken livers and the roux made with the flour. It just kind of looks "dirty." Even though this rice is anything but dirty, the name still sticks, but the taste is really what you'll remember. This side dish is a great addition to almost any Cajun meal that doesn't already contain rice. It's also good right out of the refrigerator. I like it hot or cold. Of course, you can make it in advance and refrigerate or freeze.

VEGETABLES

GREEN RICE

1 pkg. frozen broccoli
(10 oz.)
1 cup boiling water
3 tbsp. butter
1 cup onions, chopped
1 cup celery, minced
1 cup fresh mushrooms,
sliced
$^1/_2$ cup bell pepper, finely
diced
$^1/_2$ cup green onions, minced

3 cloves garlic, minced
1 can cream of chicken soup
(10$^1/_2$ oz.)
$^1/_2$ cup evaporated milk
1$^1/_2$ cup American cheese,
grated
2 cups cooked White Rice
(see index)
$^1/_2$ tsp. salt
1 tsp. black pepper
1 tsp. Tabasco® Sauce

Preheat the oven to 350 degrees. Place the frozen broccoli in a small bowl, pour the boiling water over it, and let it stand until you are ready to use. In a large, heavy skillet over medium-high heat, add the butter and let it melt. Sauté the onions, celery, mushrooms, bell pepper, green onions, and garlic for 5 minutes, stirring constantly. Add the soup and evaporated milk and mix in well, letting the mixture simmer for 3 minutes while stirring. The mixture should start to bubble. Add the cheese, rice, and broccoli that you reserved and blend together well. Season with the salt, black pepper, and Tabasco® Sauce and blend well. Pour the mixture into a 2-quart baking dish and bake at 350 degrees for 35 to 40 minutes. Serve hot. Serves 8.

Lagniappe: This is a great way to get your kids to eat broccoli. Don't tell them it's broccoli rice! It's green rice! It is truly amazing how people with an aversion to broccoli will just love this dish. Next to Dirty Rice, this is the favorite rice dish of Cajuns. This dish can be made completely and cooked in advance and refrigerated or frozen for later use. This recipe makes a wonderful side dish for almost any meal, simple or fancy. You get your starch and vegetable in one tasty dish.

BAKED SWEET POTATOES

8 large sweet potatoes, cleaned
Vegetable oil to rub on the
   skins

Butter to add after the potato
   is cooked

Preheat the oven to 425 degrees. Take each sweet potato and trim each of the ends so that the potato can "breathe" while cooking. Rub the potato lightly with the cooking oil and place on a baking pan. Put into a 425-degree oven and bake for 30 minutes, then reduce the heat to 350 degrees and continue to bake for 1 more hour or until the potato is soft. Remove from the oven and let the potato cool for 15 minutes, then cut off the peeling with a knife and place one on each serving plate. Mash the top of the potato with a fork, making somewhat of a well, and put the pat of butter in the well and serve.

Lagniappe: This is great eating! Simple but delicious. Be sure to cook the potato in its natural skin, which will allow the natural sugar in the potato to caramelize, adding to its taste. This same recipe works well to make Baked Yams that are also found in Louisiana. Both sweet potatoes and yams were discovered by the Cajuns when they arrived in the bayou country of South Louisiana. Sweet potatoes tend to be sweeter and are the long, narrow potatoes you'll find in the stores. Yams tend to be much larger. Never try to cook sweet potatoes or yams in the microwave; the fast cooking doesn't allow the natural sugars to caramelize and therefore sweeten the potato during the cooking process. This recipe takes a little time, but it is so easy. Beware, though. The smell will fill your house and make your mouth water!

SWEETS

LOUISIANA PEAR CAKE

1¹/₂ cups cooking oil
2 cups sugar
3 large eggs, slightly beaten
2¹/₂ cups flour, all-purpose
1 tsp. baking soda
2 tbsp. baking powder
1 tsp. salt
2 tsp. nutmeg
1¹/₂ tsp. cinnamon

¹/₂ tsp. ginger
3 cups Louisiana canning
    pears, cored and peeled
1 cup pecans
2 tbsp. vanilla extract
Shortening to lightly grease
    the pan (or use baker's
    spray)
¹/₂ cup sifted powdered sugar

Preheat the oven to 350 degrees. Cream the oil and sugar by whipping the oil with a stiff wire whisk and slowly add the sugar. Add the eggs and whip them in with the whisk. In another bowl, combine the flour, baking soda, baking powder, salt, nutmeg, cinnamon, and ginger; use a dry wire whisk and blend the ingredients together well. Combine the pears and the nuts in a small mixing bowl. Add the flour mixture alternately with the pears/nut mixture to the sugar and oil mixture.

When all the ingredients are combined, add the vanilla extract to the batter and mix in thoroughly. Pour the batter into a well-greased, heavy bundt pan. Bake at 350 degrees for about 1 hour. Check for doneness with a dry toothpick by piercing the center of the cake. If the toothpick comes out clean, then remove the cake. Allow the cake to cool for 10 minutes, then remove it carefully from the bundt pan by turning the cake over onto a serving plate or platter. Dust lightly with sifted powdered sugar. Serves 8 to 10.

Lagniappe: This is a very moist cake that will keep well in a covered cake plate for almost a week. That is, if you can keep people away from it for that long. I also like to use the same recipe and pour the batter into lightly greased muffin tins to make Fresh Pear Muffins. You can also use this recipe to make a wonderful Fresh Apple Cake. Just substitute 3 cups of fresh apples for the pears. Leave the peelings on the apples after you core them. I like to use 2 green Granny Smith apples and one red apple. Either way you serve this cake, it will be a hit. Louisiana canning pears can be found in much of the state and make wonderful preserves as well as this tasty dessert. You can also serve the cake with a nice dollop for fresh whipped cream.

SWEETS

BLACKBERRY COBBLER

Blackberry filling:

$^1/_2$ cup boiling water
$^1/_4$ cup cornstarch
6 cups fresh blackberries,
  washed and cleaned
$1^1/_2$ cups sugar
1 tbsp. fresh lemon juice
1 tbsp. melted butter
1 tsp. vanilla extract
$^1/_4$ tsp. salt

Cobbler pastry:

2 cups flour, all-purpose, sifted
2 tbsp. sugar
1 tsp. light brown sugar
$^1/_4$ tsp. salt
$^1/_2$ tsp. baking soda
$^3/_4$ cup shortening
$^1/_3$ cup very cold milk
Flour for dusting and keeping
  dough from sticking
2 tbsp. melted butter, unsalted
Freshly whipped cream or ice
  cream (optional)

Preheat the oven to 425 degrees. In a small mixing bowl, add the boiling water and the cornstarch. Stir together until the cornstarch dissolves. In a large glass bowl, add all the remaining filling ingredients and, using a spatula, mix them together well. Pour the cornstarch mixture on top of the berries and set the bowl aside for later use. In another metal mixing bowl, add the sifted flour, sugars, soda, and salt; blend together, using a stiff wire whisk until thoroughly mixed. Put half of the shortening into the bowl and, using the stiff wire whisk, blend it into the flour.

When finished, do the same with the remaining shortening. Slowly add the milk, one tablespoon at a time, and work it into the flour/shortening mix with the wire whisk. Continue until all the milk is added. Roll the mixture into a ball with your hands that have been lightly dusted with flour to keep the dough from sticking. Split the dough into two pieces and roll out the dough with a rolling pin on a surface lightly dusted with the flour. Roll the dough to about ¼-inch thickness.

Line the bottom and sides of a large, deep cobbler dish (10x12) with the pastry. Use a knife to cut the pastry at the top of the dish. Brush well with the melted butter. Pour the blackberry mixture onto the pie pastry. Roll the remaining half of the pastry using the same method as before. Cover the top of the baking dish with the remaining pastry, sealing the edges well all around the baking dish; crimp the edges to give character to the cobbler. Lightly butter the top pastry and cut 6, 1½-inch slits around the cobbler to allow steam to escape. Bake at 425 degrees for about 50 minutes or until the crust is nicely browned and the berries have begun to bubble around the edges. Cool and serve with freshly whipped cream or ice cream of your choice.

Lagniappe: This is a taste-tempting treat using the blackberries that grow wild all over South Louisiana. This was always a treat we could look for after spending the day on the side of the road and in the pastures around the house picking buckets of blackberries. Today there are many new cultured varieties that are quite good as well, but going out and picking your own berries in the "wild" was a thrill for most young Cajuns.

If you can keep your family members away from the cobbler, you can freeze it for later use. Mom always made two or three cobblers so we could freeze a few for wonderful treats outside of blackberry season. Be sure to tightly wrap the cobbler, using that new plastic wrap that seals itself, before freezing. Enjoy!

SWEETS

BREAD PUDDING

For the pudding:

15 slices bread or 1 large loaf
   of French bread
1 can (13 oz.) evaporated milk
2½ cups milk
1 stick butter, unsalted, cut
   into pieces
5 large eggs, well beaten
2 cups sugar
1 large Granny Smith apple,
   peeled and diced
1 pkg. (10 oz.) frozen sweet-
   ened peaches, chopped
½ cup raisins
½ cup golden raisins

⅔ cup pecans, chopped
1 tsp. allspice
1 tsp. nutmeg
1½ tsp. cinnamon
1 tbsp. vanilla extract
Butter to grease the pudding
   pan
Water for baking pan

For the whisky sauce:

1 cup sugar
½ cup whisky
1 stick butter, unsalted
2 large eggs, well beaten

Preheat the oven to 350 degrees. Tear the bread into
pieces and place in a large glass bowl. In a saucepan over
low heat, combine the evaporated milk, regular milk, and
butter. Heat until the butter is melted and the milk is hot,
about 5 minutes over low heat. Pour over the bread and
mix well. Let it stand for 10 minutes, then add the eggs,
sugar, apple, peaches, raisins, and pecans. Blend well. Add
the allspice, nutmeg, cinnamon, and vanilla, then mix
together very well.

Pour into a lightly greased, ovenproof baking dish
(10x14) and set this pan into a larger baking dish that has
1 inch of water in it. Bake at 350 degrees for about 1
hour or until a knife inserted into the center of the pudding comes out clean. Remove carefully from the oven

and let it stand for 15 minutes, then serve hot or cold with Whisky Sauce on top or on the side.

To make the Whisky Sauce, cook the sugar, whisky, and butter in a double boiler until very hot and the sugar is well dissolved. Remove from the heat, add the egg, and whip together very fast so that the egg doesn't curdle. Return the double boiler to the heat and cook, stirring constantly, for 3 minutes or until the sauce has thickened. Let the sauce cool for 3 minutes, then spoon on top of the cut bread pudding. Serves 10 to 12.

Lagniappe: A great dessert that was created to find a use for old, stale bread. This is a dish that is great after any meal or as a night-time snack. My grandmother used to make bread pudding almost every week. She always liked to have sweets around the house, and she never liked to waste anything. So bread pudding was just the dish to achieve both these objectives.

You can make this pudding in advance and refrigerate or freeze. It is almost always better after two or three days. The flavors tend to blend with a little refrigeration. To reheat, just take the individual size you want for a serving and either heat in the microwave or heat in a 300 degree oven for 15 minutes. You can serve with Whisky Sauce, Brandy Sauce, Rum Sauce, or with a nice topping of freshly made whipped cream. To make Brandy Sauce or Rum Sauce, just substitute equal amounts of either brandy or rum in place of the whisky.

CARROT CAKE

Cake:

2 cups flour, all-purpose
2 cups sugar
$^{1}/_{2}$ cup brown sugar
2 tsp. baking powder
2 tsp. baking soda
2 tsp. cinnamon
1 tsp. nutmeg
$^{1}/_{4}$ tsp. ginger
1 tsp. salt
1 cup pecans or walnuts,
    chopped
4 large eggs, slightly beaten
2 large eggs, yolks only,
    slightly beaten
1$^{1}/_{2}$ cups cooking oil
3$^{1}/_{2}$ cups carrots, finely grated
Butter for greasing the baking
    pans
Flour for dusting the pans

Frosting:

1 stick butter, unsalted,
    softened
1 pkg. (8 oz.) cream cheese,
    softened
3 cups powdered sugar
1$^{1}/_{2}$ tsp. vanilla extract
1 cup pecans or walnuts,
    chopped

Preheat the oven to 325 degrees. In a large mixing bowl, mix together all the ingredients for the cake except the eggs, oil, carrots, butter, and flour for dusting. Use a wire whisk for blending it all together. In another bowl, cream the eggs, yolks, and cooking oil until it is very well blended. Pour the creamed eggs into the dry ingredients and mix well. Fold in the carrots until the batter is smooth and well blended.

Lightly grease three cake pans (9-inch), then lightly dust them with the flour. Pour equal amounts of the carrot batter into each pan. Bake for 45 minutes or until the cakes have risen nicely and are well browned. Check for doneness by inserting a toothpick into the center of the cake; it should come out clean. If not, bake for 5 more minutes and repeat the test. Remove from the oven and let cool while you make the frosting.

In a medium mixing bowl, cream the cream cheese and butter until light and fluffy. Add the sugar, vanilla, and pecans a little at a time until all is used. Spread the frosting between each layer of cake and on the top of the last layer. Allow to sit 15 minutes for the frosting to set. Serves 8 to 10.

Lagniappe: What a way to eat carrots! Carrots were such a staple crop of the early Cajuns that it is no wonder they developed a recipe to eat them in other ways. This is a tempting dessert that will please your family or guests. You can use this exact recipe and substitute grated zucchini for carrots to make Zucchini Cake, or you can substitute grated yellow squash for the carrots to make Summer Squash Cake. These are interesting and exciting ways to eat your vegetable and cake, too!

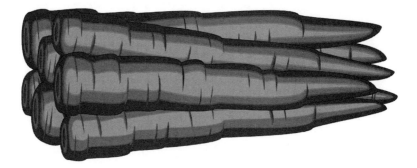

COOKED CUSTARD

4 large eggs
1 cup sugar
2 cups evaporated milk

4 cups milk
1 tsp. vanilla extract
$\frac{1}{4}$ tsp. nutmeg

Preheat the oven to 300 degrees. Beat the eggs until they are stiff, add the sugar, and beat until it is all incorporated. Add the evaporated milk, regular milk, vanilla, and nutmeg and beat until it is well blended. Pour into two $1\frac{1}{2}$-quart baking dishes. Place the dishes in a 300-degree oven in two pans of shallow water. Close the oven door and raise the temperature to 400 degrees. Cook for about 1 hour or until the custard is set. Check with a knife inserted into the center of the custard; if the knife comes out clean, the custard is done. Let the custard cool and serve. Serves 8 to 10.

Lagniappe: This is old-time custard that Grandma used to make. It is simple and easy, but the taste is delightful. You can cook in individual ramekin dishes if you like. I also like to dot the custard with a bit of freshly whipped cream. It's hard to believe that something this simple can taste so delicious. It makes for a great ending to almost any dinner or lunch.

You can refrigerate until you are ready to serve, or you can store leftovers for up to 4 days. You can also add slices of fresh fruit to your plate when you serve the custard.

SWEETS

DATE NUT ROLL

2 cups sugar
1 cup evaporated milk
1 cup dates, chopped

1 cup pecans, chopped
1 tsp. vanilla extract

In a heavy, medium saucepan over medium heat, cook the sugar and evaporated milk to the soft-ball stage, about 12 to 14 minutes. Add the dates and continue to cook until it forms a hard ball, about 8 to 10 more minutes. Stir constantly, then remove from the heat and add the pecans and vanilla extract. Beat the mixture until it is very thick. Pour it out onto a damp cloth and roll it into a log, about 12 to 16 inches long and $1^1/_2$ inches thick. Put into the refrigerator and chill for 25 minutes. Unroll the cloth and cut the log into $^1/_4$-inch circles. Makes about 3 dozen pieces. Excellent for snacks, especially during the winter holidays.

Lagniappe: This is a unique treat from the bayou country of New Iberia. This was a favorite of my wife's aunt. It is a recipe handed down from generation to generation. It's simple, but quite tasty. You can store the candies for up to 1 month in a tightly covered dry container. It's a wonderful snack candy and great for company visits.

LOUISIANA MUD CAKE

For the cake:

4 large eggs
2 cups sugar
2 sticks butter, melted
1 1/2 cups flour
1/2 cup cocoa
1 cup pecans, chopped
1 tsp. vanilla
Shortening for greasing pan
Flour for dusting pan
1 large jar marshmallow
    cream

For the icing:

1 stick butter
6 tbsp. milk
1 box (1 lb.) powdered sugar
1 tsp. vanilla extract
1 cup pecans, chopped

Preheat the oven to 350 degrees. Beat the eggs and sugar together until they are thick, about 5 minutes. In another mixing bowl, combine the melted butter, flour, cocoa, pecans, and vanilla together; blend well. Add this flour mixture to the egg and sugar mixture and blend together until it is well mixed. Pour the batter into a greased flour pan (9x13) that has been lightly dusted with flour. Bake for 30 minutes at 350 degrees. Remove from the oven and spread the jar of marshmallow cream on top of the cake while it is hot. Allow the cake to cool while you make the icing.

Melt the butter over low heat in a small saucepan. Remove the pan from the heat and add the milk, sugar, and vanilla. Beat together well. Add the nuts and mix them in evenly. Spread this icing over the marshmallow cream on the top of the Louisiana Mud Cake. Allow the icing to set, then serve. Serves 8 to 10.

Lagniappe: All I can say is wow! This cake gets its name from the mud along the bayous of Louisiana. But it's anything but muddy! This is a cake that will keep them coming back. It's easy, but so delicious. This will be the cake that you take to your company dinners.

OREILLES DE COCHON (PIG EARS-SHAPED PASTRY)

$^1/_2$ stick butter, unsalted
1 large egg, well beaten
2 cups flour, all-purpose
$1^1/_2$ tsp. baking powder
$^1/_2$ tsp. salt

Cooking oil for deep frying
2 cups cane syrup
1 tbsp. molasses
1 cup pecans, chopped

Mix the butter and eggs together in a mixing bowl. Combine the flour, baking powder, and salt in another bowl. Slowly, about $^1/_2$ cup at a time, add the flour to the butter mixture, stirring after each addition. The dough will be easy to handle.

Separate the dough into sixteen 1-inch balls. On a lightly floured surface, roll each of the balls into a thin circle about 4 to 6 inches in diameter. Pour about 3 inches of oil into a deep-fat fryer and heat the oil to 350 degrees. Fry the circles, one at a time. Using a fork, twist one side of the circle to give it a swirl and make it look somewhat like a pig's ear. When the "ear" is light brown, remove and drain on a paper towel. Repeat the process until all the ears are fried. Set them aside while you make the topping.

In a small saucepan over medium heat, cook the syrup and the molasses until the syrup reaches the soft-ball stage. Add the pecans and cook for 2 more minutes. Drizzle the syrup/pecan topping over the ears and serve either warm or cool. Makes 16 large ears or cakes. Serve as a dessert or as a snack.

Lagniappe: This is an old Acadian treat. Oreilles de cochon, or course, is Cajun French for pig ears. You can make the oreilles one or two days in advance. Just keep them tightly covered in a cool, dry place. Try not to put them on top of each other because they will have a tendency to break apart. They are much better served the day you make them.

PECAN PRALINES

4 cups sugar
$1/2$ cup light brown sugar
$1/2$ cup water
1 cup evaporated milk
$1/2$ tsp. salt
4 cups pecans, broken into
  pieces

1 stick butter, unsalted
2 tsp. vanilla extract
Buttered platter to pour out
  the pralines or use a platter
  covered with wax paper

Mix the sugar, brown sugar, water, evaporated milk, and salt in a medium-size, heavy saucepan and bring the mixture to a boil over medium-high heat. When the mixture begins to boil, reduce the heat to low and cook, stirring constantly, until a soft ball forms when a small amount of mixture is dropped into cold water. Add the pecans and cook for 3 more minutes.

Remove from the heat and add the butter and vanilla and stir vigorously for 1 minute. Then drop about 2 tablespoons at a time onto a buttered platter or platter covered with wax paper. Let the pralines harden, then store in a tightly covered container in a cool dry place. Makes about 35 pralines.

Lagniappe: Pralines will easily keep for a week without any loss of texture or flavor and are an excellent candy or dessert. This is the Cajun recipe for making this old French candy. The original candy was made with almonds. Almonds were not in as ample supply as the native Louisiana pecans and therefore a new praline was born. Cajuns often used canned milk to make dishes that previously were made with heavy cream. This praline is different from the praline you find in New Orleans.

PECAN PIE

2 large eggs, beaten
1 large egg, yolk only
¹/₂ cup dark corn syrup
¹/₂ cup light corn syrup
1 cup sugar
1 tbsp. flour, all-purpose

¹/₂ tsp. salt
1 stick butter, melted
1 tbsp. vanilla extract
1¹/₂ cups pecans, half broken, half whole
1 deep dish unbaked pie shell

Preheat the oven to 350 degrees. In a small mixing bowl, beat together the eggs and corn syrup until well mixed. In a large mixing bowl, add the sugar, flour, and salt and mix together well. Pour the egg/corn syrup mixture into the flour mixture and add the butter and vanilla; blend well. Pour in the pecans and mix in until well blended. Pour the pecan mixture into the pie shell. Place on a baking sheet and bake in the center of the oven for 1 hour and 5 minutes or until the pie has set. Remove from the oven and let the pie cool before serving. Serve warm or at room temperature.

Lagniappe: During pecan season, you'll find all types of pecan dishes in Louisiana. Pecan pie is always a favorite. Some people like to make Fig-Pecan Pie by adding ¹/₂ cup of fig preserves and 1 egg, beaten to the egg/corn syrup mixture above. Then follow the recipe. Another great pecan pie is Sweet Potato Pecan Pie. To make this pie, just add 1 cup of cooked and mashed sweet potatoes to the egg/corn syrup mixture above along with another whole egg, slightly beaten. Add ¹/₂ teaspoon of nutmeg to the bowl with the sugar and flour and blend in well. Continue to make the pie as directed above. No matter which pecan pie you choose to make, it will turn out to be a hit!

PECAN CAKE

To make the cake:

¹/₂ cup vegetable
  shortening
1¹/₂ cups sugar
2 large eggs, beaten
1 tsp. vanilla extract
2 cups cake flour
2¹/₂ tsp. baking powder
¹/₂ tsp. baking soda
1 tsp. salt
1 cup milk
1 tbsp. water
2 buttered and lightly floured
  cake pans (9-inch, round)

To make the cake frosting:

1¹/₂ cups sugar
¹/₂ cup light corn syrup
¹/₄ cup water
4 large eggs, whites only
¹/₂ tsp. cream of tartar
2 tsp. vanilla extract

To make the pecan filling:

1 stick butter, unsalted
1 cup sugar
1 tbsp. flour, all-purpose
2 cups light brown sugar
¹/₄ cup evaporated milk
3 large eggs, yolks only, well
  beaten
1¹/₂ cups pecans, broken
2 tsp. vanilla extract

Preheat the oven to 375 degrees. In a mixing bowl, cream the shortening until it is soft and fluffy. Add the sugar, ¹/₂ cup at a time, creaming thoroughly after each addition. Add the eggs and vanilla and beat well until the mixture is well blended and smooth. In another mixing bowl, combine the flour, baking powder, baking soda, and salt and blend well together. Add one-third of the flour at a time to the sugar mixture alternately with one-third of the milk at a time, blending well after each addition until the batter is smooth. Continue until all the flour and milk is used. Add the water and blend in until the batter is light, airy, and smooth.

Pour into the two greased and floured cake pans. Bake at 375 degrees for 25 minutes or until a toothpick inserted into the middle of the cakes comes out clean. Let the cakes cool before you remove them from the pans. Set aside while you make the filling.

To make the filling, add the butter to a large saucepan over low heat and let it melt. Mix together the sugar, flour, and brown sugar until well blended in a small mixing bowl, then add the sugars/flour mixture, milk, and egg yolks to the skillet; stir well. Cook over low heat for 5 minutes. Add $1/2$ cup of the pecans and cook for 2 more minutes. Remove from the heat and add the remaining pecans and the vanilla; beat together well. Let the mixture cool while you take the cakes out of the cake pans. Place one on a cake plate and spoon half of the pecan mixture on top of it. Place the other cake half on top of the first and cover with the remaining pecan filling. Set the cake aside while you make the frosting.

To make the frosting, add the sugar, corn syrup, and water to a medium saucepan over medium heat and bring to a hard boil. While the sugar is cooking, beat the egg whites, cream of tartar, and vanilla until stiff peaks form. When the sugar mixture begins to boil, let it boil for 2 minutes, then reduce the heat to a low boil. Continue to cook the mixture until a drop of the sugar put into a cup of cold water forms a hard ball.

When the boiling sugar has reached this stage, begin beating the eggs again and drizzle the hot mixture a little at a time into the beaten egg whites until all the hot syrup mixture is used. Be sure to beat constantly. The frosting should form stiff peaks. Spread this frosting on the cake you have set aside. You can decorate the top of the cake with pecan halves.

Lagniappe: This is a prize cake. It celebrates the pecan. Be sure to have the cake baked and the filling on the cake before you begin making the frosting. This frosting needs to be put on the cake right after it is prepared. This is the Sunday cake recipe that my grandmother used to make. It was a family favorite. Today, I have to make it for all family gatherings. It brings back the feeling that we all had when Grams was with us. While there are a lot of steps to this cake, it really isn't hard to make. It just takes time and lots of love!

RICE PUDDING

2 cups milk
1¹/₄ cups sugar
¹/₄ cup light brown sugar,
   packed
4 large brown eggs, lightly
   beaten
1 med. apple, finely diced
¹/₂ cups raisins
¹/₂ cup pineapple, crushed
¹/₂ tsp. ginger
1 tsp. nutmeg
¹/₂ tsp. cinnamon
1 cup cooked White Rice (see
   index)
Water for baking pan
2 cups freshly whipped heavy
   cream with 2 tbsp. of sugar
   added

Preheat the oven to 325 degrees. Pour the milk into a heavy saucepan over medium heat and bring it to a boil. Reduce the heat to low once it begins to boil and let the milk simmer until the milk is scalded. Mix the sugar, brown sugar, and eggs until well creamed in a large mixing bowl. Pour the scalded milk on top of the sugar/egg mixture and blend together well. Add the apple, raisins, pineapple, spices, and rice, then thoroughly blend until well mixed.

Pour the pudding into a shallow, 2¹/₂-quart baking dish and place the dish in a large baking pan with 1 inch of water in it. Bake at 325 degrees for 1 hour or until a knife inserted into the center comes out clean. Remove carefully from the oven and let the pudding cool for 15 to 20 minutes before serving. You can refrigerate if you prefer the pudding chilled. It's great either warm or cold. Serve with a half cup of freshly whipped cream on top. Serves 8.

Lagniappe: Do not freeze this pudding. You can bake the pudding ahead of time and refrigerate until you are ready to serve. It will keep in the refrigerator for up to 3 days. Serve it cold or heat it in the oven at 300 degrees for 5 to

7 minutes and serve warm. Individual servings also heat well in the microwave at 70 percent power for about 30 seconds. Rice is a Cajun staple, and it was only a matter of time before the Cajuns put it into a dessert! This is basically a bread pudding made with rice instead of bread.

SWEET POTATO PIE

For pie shell:

1 cup shortening
1 tbsp. sugar
2 tsp. vinegar
3 cups sifted flour, all-purpose
1 tsp. salt
Ice water
Lightly floured surface for
   rolling pie crust

For the filling:

1$^1/_2$ cups cooked Sweet
   Potatoes, mashed (see index)
$^1/_2$ cup half and half cream
$^1/_2$ cup butter, melted
3 large eggs, well beaten
$^1/_2$ tsp. baking powder
1 tsp. nutmeg
1 tsp. vanilla extract
$^1/_4$ tsp. ginger
1 tsp. grated lemon rind
$^1/_2$ tsp. salt
1 cup sugar
$^1/_4$ cup brown sugar

Preheat the oven to 400 degrees. To make the pie shell, in a large mixing bowl cream the sugar and vinegar with the shortening until the shortening is smooth and soft. Mix the salt into the flour and add the flour to the shortening mix and knead it together with your hands. Add enough ice water to allow the dough to form a nice ball. Place the rounded dough onto the lightly floured surface and roll the dough into a large circle about $^1/_4$ inch thick. Place the dough on top of a 9-inch pie plate and cut it to fit. Crimp the edges to add character to the pie shell.

To make the filling, in another large mixing bowl add all the ingredients and mix together very well until the batter is smooth and creamy. Pour into the pie shell and bake at 400 degrees for about 35 minutes or until the pie has set and is golden brown. Serve warm or chilled.

Lagniappe: This is another staple in Cajun Louisiana. Sweet potatoes are plentiful in the state and were growing wild when the Cajuns arrived in the bayous. Potatoes and yams were plants that were native to America and were part of the bounty that this country gave to the world. They keep well, allowing them to be utilized as an ingredient for cooking much of the year. This pie can be made in advance and refrigerated until you are ready to serve. It will keep for 5 days refrigerated. It is still best right from the oven. I like to make a fresh, heavy whipped cream to serve with it; it brings out the sweetness of the pie and add to its delicate flavor.

TEA CAKES

2 cups sugar	1 tsp. vanilla extract
1 stick butter	3 1/2 cups flour, all-purpose
1/2 cup buttermilk	1/2 tsp. baking soda
2 large eggs, beaten (brown	2 tsp. baking powder
eggs are best for this recipe)	1 tsp. salt
2 tsp. finely grated lemon rind	1 tsp. cream of tartar

Preheat the oven to 375 degrees. Cream together the sugar, butter, buttermilk, eggs, lemon rind, and vanilla until smooth. Mix together the flour, baking soda, baking powder, salt, and cream of tartar until well blended, then sift the dry ingredients a little at a time into the creamed egg/butter mixture. Mix until the dough is stiff enough to roll. Roll on a floured surface to about $3/8$ inch thick and cut with a large biscuit cutter. Place on a lightly buttered cookie sheet and bake at 375 degrees for about 10 minutes or until the edges of the cookie are a golden brown. Makes about 36 tea cakes.

Lagniappe: This is a simple cookie that was such a treat when I was a kid. My grandmother used to keep tea cakes in a big jar in her kitchen. They were always a delight. These cookies will keep in a tightly covered container for one week, if you can keep people away from them!

SWEETS

SEASONING MIXES, SAUCES, BREAKFAST DISHES, AND MISCELLANEOUS

CAJUN SEASONING MIX

$^1/_4$ cup salt
$^1/_4$ cup paprika
3 tbsp. cayenne pepper
2 tbsp. onion powder
$1^1/_2$ tbsp. garlic powder
$1^1/_2$ tbsp. fresh ground black
   pepper
1 tbsp. white pepper
2 tsp. dried sweet basil
2 tsp. chili powder
1 tsp. dry hot mustard

$^1/_2$ tsp. ground bay leaves
$^1/_2$ tsp. filé powder
$^1/_2$ tsp. ground cloves
$^1/_4$ tsp. ground thyme
$^1/_4$ tsp. rosemary
$^1/_4$ tsp. ground ginger
$^1/_4$ tsp. cumin powder
$^1/_8$ tsp. ground allspice
$^1/_8$ tsp. ground nutmeg
$^1/_8$ tsp. ground tarragon

Combine all the ingredients in a mixing bowl and mix thoroughly with a wire whisk. Store in a tightly covered glass jar for use as needed.

Lagniappe: This is a general Cajun seasoning mix. You can almost say this recipe is the only one you need to do genuine Cajun cooking. If you have to watch your salt on any diet you may be on, feel free to cut down on the salt according to your specific needs. If you are on a salt-free diet, just cut out all of the salt and use the rest of the recipe as an excellent seasoning. You can store this seasoning mix in a cool dry place for up to 4 months without losing its flavor and freshness. This seasoning mix makes a great Christmas gift or special thank-you gift throughout the year.

HOLLANDAISE SAUCE

1 stick butter, unsalted
4 large eggs, yolks only
$^1/_4$ cup lemon juice, freshly
    squeezed
$^1/_2$ tsp. Tabasco® Sauce

$^1/_2$ tsp. white pepper
$^1/_2$ tsp. salt
1 tsp. cold water
1 tbsp. cold butter, cut into
    small pieces

Melt the stick of butter over low heat and set it aside, keeping it warm, not hot. In a heavy metal mixing bowl, place the egg yolks and whip them briskly with a limber wire whisk until they have increased their volume and become thickened. Add the lemon juice, Tabasco® Sauce, white pepper, and salt and whip together well until the mixture is well mixed. Boil water in a saucepan that is small enough for the bottom of the metal bowl to rest on it. When the water is boiling, reduce the heat to a rolling simmer (just a little steam should rise) and place the metal bowl on top of the saucepan. Continue to whisk the mixture for about 3 to 4 minutes, constantly scraping the sides so that the egg mixture won't stick or scramble.

When the mixture is thick (like pudding), add the cold water and cold tablespoon of butter pieces, then begin drizzling the melted butter into the sauce, while constantly beating. Make sure you keep your hand on the bowl. If the bowl gets too hot for you to touch, then it is too hot for the eggs and they will scramble. If the bowl gets to hot to touch, remove from the heat for a few seconds, then lower it back again as it cools. The sauce is ready when all the butter is blended and the mixture is thick and smooth. Makes about 1 cup of sauce. Keep at room temperature until ready to serve.

Lagniappe: This is a sauce that should be made as it is needed. If you do happen to have some left over, don't throw it out. Simply store it in the refrigerator in a tightly covered bowl. When you are ready to use it, let it stand at room temperature for about 15 minutes, then whip it with a fork or wire whisk. It will regain some of its consistency and although the flavor and texture are somewhat altered, by no means will the sauce be tasteless.

When the sauce is freshly made, do not let it stand for more than 15 to 20 minutes at room temperature to be sure that it is safely handled. This is egg yolks, and even though lemon juice will help prevent the growth of bacteria, you should not leave this sauce out for too long, so make it just before you need it. This sauce is wonderful over vegetables, meats, poached fish, chicken, and eggs.

Use this same recipe to make Bearnaise Sauce with these few changes. In a small saucepan, add $\frac{1}{2}$ cup of white wine vinegar, $\frac{1}{2}$ cup of Vermouth wine, 1 tablespoon of shallots, finely minced, and $\frac{1}{2}$ teaspoon of tarragon. Bring the mixture to a boil and let it simmer until the liquid has reduced to about $\frac{1}{3}$ cup. Use this liquid instead of the lemon juice and follow the directions as above to make a delicious Bearnaise Sauce. Bearnaise is perfect as a sauce for steaks and broiled fish or on eggs.

You can also use this recipe for hollandaise to make a fine Mousseline Sauce by simply whipping $\frac{1}{2}$ cup of heavy whipping cream until stiff peaks form. Fold this whipped cream into the Hollandaise Sauce until it is completely mixed. This is an excellent sauce for chicken, fish, vegetables, or casseroles. It is a much lighter hollandaise and has a wonderful airy texture.

DARK BROWN ROUX

1¼ cups cooking oil   A little water, if needed
1 cup flour, all-purpose

In a heavy metal pot over medium high heat, warm the oil until it is hot, then sprinkle the flour into the pot. Heat, stirring constantly (I like to use a flexible wire whisk), until the flour turns a dark, rich reddish brown. Be careful not to let any of the flour stick, and do not stop stirring.

When the color is correct (not black, but a very dark reddish brown), remove from the heat and continue to stir until the roux cools. You can add a small amount of water to help cool down the roux, but be careful because the hot mixture will splatter when you put the water in it. When the roux is cooled, you can store it in the refrigerator for later use as needed.

Lagniappe: Roux will keep tightly stored in the refrigerator for up to one month. You can also freeze it if you want to keep it longer. Use this roux to add body and richness to most dishes that have a gravy or to rice dressings or any casseroles to help thicken and intensify their flavors. If you want to use it right after making, you can simply add the vegetables you plan on sautéing in your recipe right after the desired color of the roux is reached. Generally, you'd add chopped onions, bell pepper, celery and garlic to help create a wonderful Cajun flavor for any dish that has a gravy. The roux not only thickens the sauce, but it intensifies the sauce's flavor as well. It acts as a "flavor sponge" and imparts that flavor throughout your finished dish.

HEAVY CREAM SAUCE

1 stick butter, unsalted
$^1/_2$ cup flour, all-purpose
1 tsp. salt
1 tsp. Tabasco® Sauce

$^1/_2$ tsp. white pepper
1 cup half and half cream
$^1/_2$ cup heavy whipping cream

In a medium saucepan over low heat, melt the butter. Slowly blend in the flour, salt, Tabasco® Sauce, and white pepper. Cook, stirring constantly, over low heat for 5 minutes or until the mixture is smooth and somewhat bubbly. Do not let the flour brown! Remove the pan from the heat and slowly add the half and half; stir with a wire whisk until the mixture is smooth. Add the heavy whipping cream and blend in well. Return to the low heat and cook until the sauce thickens and is smooth, about 2 to 3 minutes. Remove from the heat. Makes about 2 cups of sauce.

Lagniappe: This is a great sauce to use on vegetables, egg dishes, casseroles, or seafood. It is also an excellent "base" sauce to which you can add cheese to make a wonderful Mornay Sauce. Just add the $^2/_3$ cup of grated cheese (American, Cheddar, Swiss, or Monterrey Jack) to the sauce and stir until the cheese has melted. Mornay sauce is great on top of steamed vegetables, poultry, fish or pork.

To make a Veloute Sauce, just add $^1/_4$ cup of meat juice or fish juice obtained from the cooking of the meat or fish. Reduce $^1/_4$ cup of the half and half cream and substitute the juice from the pan while cooking your entrée. This will add flavor to your entrée and bring together the flavors of the dish and the excitement of an outstanding sauce. Of course, you'd use this sauce on the dish you take the juice from and on vegetables served with your main course.

To make a Bechamel Sauce, use the recipe for the Heavy Cream Sauce and just change the name to Bechamel Sauce. They are one in the same! Bechamel is the proper French culinary name for a heavy cream sauce.

MARCHAND DE VIN SAUCE

3/4 cup butter, unsalted
1 cup mushrooms, finely
    chopped
2/3 cup ham, minced
1/3 cup shallots, finely
    chopped
1/2 cup onions, finely chopped
1/4 cup bell pepper, finely
    diced

4 cloves garlic, crushed then
    finely minced
2 tbsp. flour, all-purpose
1 tsp. salt
1 tsp. white pepper
1/2 tsp. cayenne pepper
3/4 cup Beef Stock (see index)
1/2 cup dry red wine
1 tsp. Tabasco® Sauce

Melt the butter in a medium saucepan over medium-high heat and lightly sauté the mushrooms, ham, shallots, onions, bell pepper, and garlic. When the onion is a golden brown, after about 5 minutes, add the flour, salt, white pepper, and cayenne. Brown the flour well, about 10 minutes, stirring constantly. Blend in the stock, wine, and Tabasco® Sauce and simmer over very low heat for about 30 minutes, stirring now and then to prevent sticking. Makes about 2 1/2 cups of sauce.

Lagniappe: This sauce is excellent over any red meat, some poultry dishes, and on poached eggs. You can simply broil a steak or grill it and add this sauce to make an easy main dish. The sauce is also delicious over broiled chicken breasts. As another option, poached eggs can be placed on toast points and covered generously with this sauce to make a creative breakfast dish. The sauce is also a fine base sauce that stew meat can be simmered in to create a tasty Beef Stew Marchand de Vin. Simply brown 2 pounds of beef stew that has been seasoned with 2 teaspoons of Cajun Seasoning Mix for 5 minutes or until well browned. Add the stew meat to a heavy skillet that has a cover and pour the Marchand de Vin Sauce on top, stir, and cover. Simmer the stew for 1 hour over low heat, covered. An easy but delightful dish.

REMOULADE SAUCE

4 cloves garlic, finely minced
1/2 cup fresh parsley, finely minced
1 cup celery, finely chopped
1 1/2 cups green onions, minced
3 tbsp. bell pepper, finely minced
4 tbsp. Creole mustard
1 tbsp. Dijon-style mustard
2 tbsp. prepared horseradish
2 tbsp. paprika
1 tsp. salt
1 tsp. black pepper, freshly ground
1 tsp. Tabasco® Sauce
1/2 tsp. white pepper
1/2 tsp. cayenne pepper
1 tsp. onion powder
1/2 tsp. garlic powder
2 tsp. sugar
2 tbsp. red wine vinegar
1 tbsp. Balsamic vinegar
1/3 cup distilled white vinegar
2/3 cup olive oil, extra virgin

Add all the ingredients except the last two to a food processor and blend at high speed for 2 minutes. The mixture should be well blended. Add the white vinegar and blend at high speed for 1 more minute. Leave the processor running and remove the piece that lets you add ingredients while the blender is running. Slowly drizzle the olive oil into the processor until it is all used. Remove the sauce from the processor and place in a large metal bowl; tightly cover and refrigerate for 4 hours. Spoon this sauce on top or boiled of broiled seafood or serve with raw oysters. Makes about 3 cups of sauce.

Lagniappe: Not only can this sauce be made in advance and refrigerated for up to 4 days, but this storage time also seems to improve the flavor. Do not freeze this sauce! It is also an excellent salad dressing. Just serve as you would any dressing.

To serve as an appetizer, place the boiled or broiled seafood of your choice on a bed of shredded lettuce leaves and spoon generous amounts of the sauce on top. You can use this recipe to make Shrimp Remoulade. Place 6 to 8 boiled or broiled shrimp, peeled and deveined, in a serving dish that has a bed of lettuce in it. Cover with $1/4$ cup of Remoulade Sauce. To make Crawfish Remoulade, place 15 to 20 peeled crawfish tails in a serving dish covered with Remoulade Sauce or place the crawfish on a bed of lettuce and cover with the sauce. To make Crabmeat Remoulade, place about $1/3$ cup of all-lump crabmeat on a bed of shredded lettuce leaves and cover with the Remoulade Sauce. Use the sauce with fresh oysters to make Oysters Remoulade. You can either put the oysters in a serving dish and cover with remoulade or place the oysters in the sauce.

CAJUN SEAFOOD COCKTAIL SAUCE

1 cup catsup
1/2 cup chili sauce
3 tbsp. prepared horseradish
1 1/2 tsp. Tabasco® Sauce
1/2 cup celery, finely minced
3 cloves garlic, minced
1/2 cup green onions, minced

2 tbsp. fresh parsley, minced
1 tsp. salt
1 tbsp. Worcestershire sauce
1/2 tsp. sweet basil
1/2 tsp. ground bay leaf
3 tbsp. lemon juice, freshly
  squeezed

Mix all the ingredients together well in a mixing bowl. Cover and let stand in the refrigerator for 3 to 4 hours before using. Makes about 2 cups of sauce.

Lagniappe: Make this sauce up to 3 days in advance and refrigerate until ready to use. It is an excellent sauce for any boiled, broiled, or grilled seafood. It is also a wonderful sauce for fresh raw oysters. You can place the raw oysters in the sauce or serve it on top. Use as a dipping sauce for seafood or spoon it over the seafood. For oysters, you can place the raw oysters into the sauce or serve it on top. No matter how you choose to use it, it is tasty and enhances the flavors of the seafood.

Use this recipe to make Shrimp Cocktail by placing 6 to 8 boiled or broiled shrimp that have been peeled and deveined on a bed of shredded lettuce leaves. Cover with a generous serving of the cocktail sauce. To make Lump Crabmeat Cocktail, use about 1/3 cup of all-lump crabmeat placed on a bed of shredded lettuce leaves and cover with about 1/3 cup of cocktail sauce. For Crawfish Cocktail, place 1/2 cup of peeled and deveined crawfish tails on a bed of shredded lettuce and cover with 1/2 cup of cocktail sauce. Finally, use this sauce with Oysters on the Half Shell, or place 6 raw oysters in a cocktail dish and cover them with $^1/_2$ cup of cocktail sauce to make a very good Oyster Cocktail. Garnish all the cocktail with wedges of freshly cut lemons or limes.

SEASONING MIXES. SAUCES. BREAKFAST

TARTAR SAUCE

2 cups Mayonnaise (see index) or store-bought mayonnaise
$^1/_4$ cup onions, minced
$^1/_8$ cup celery, finely minced
1 tbsp. fresh parsley, finely minced
2 tbsp. green onions, finely minced
1 tbsp. fresh lemon juice
1 tsp. Tabasco® Sauce
1 tsp. salt
$^1/_4$ cup sweet pickle relish
$^1/_2$ tsp. hot dry mustard
$^1/_2$ tsp. cream of tartar
2 large boiled eggs, yolks only, finely chopped
1 tbsp. capers, chopped

Mix all the ingredients together until well mixed. Cover and refrigerate for at least 2 hours. Keeps in the refrigerator for up to 1 week. Makes about 3 cups of sauce.

Lagniappe: Excellent with fried or broiled seafood. Great with fried catfish! This is an easy sauce, but it adds so much flavor to the seafood it accompanies. You can also change the sweet pickle relish to dill pickle relish and increase the amount of capers by 3 tablespoons if you like your tartar to have a dill, pungent taste. I also like to finely chop the boiled egg whites and add them to the sauce for a different taste. Some people like to add Creole mustard or prepared Dijon-style mustard to the sauce as a matter of personal preference. Try the alternatives to see which is your favorite.

PAIN PERDU

3 large eggs, well beaten
1/2 cup sugar
1 tsp. cinnamon
1 tsp. nutmeg
1/4 tsp. allspice
1/4 tsp. salt

2 tsp. vanilla extract
1 tsp. fresh lemon juice
3/4 cup milk
8 slices stale bread
1/3 cup cooking oil
1/2 cup powdered sugar

In a large mixing bowl, cream the eggs and sugar together. Add the cinnamon, nutmeg, allspice, salt, vanilla, and lemon juice and blend in well until mixed. Slowly beat in the milk with a wire whisk until all the milk is used. Place the slices of bread into the bowl, one at a time, and let the bread soak up the egg mixture on each side.

Heat the cooking oil in a large, heavy skillet over medium-low heat until it is hot. Fry each slice of bread until it has browned nicely on each side. Serve warm, right from the skillet, sprinkled with a little powdered sugar. Serves 4.

Lagniappe: Pain Perdu (bread lost) is the Louisiana version of French toast. Do not make in advance; prepare just before you plan to serve. It is possible to freeze Pain Perdu, but I am not really thrilled with the results. And it is so simple to make that the only possible reason to freeze it would be when you have large amounts of stale bread and not enough people to feed breakfast to the next day.

It is necessary to use stale bread because fresh bread just tears apart too easily. Some people like to serve warm cane syrup or maple syrup with the Pain Perdu, so if you'd like to try syrup with it, feel free. I just think it is too good to add anything to it. Bread was too hard to come by for the Cajuns to throw away, so like many excellent Cajun dishes, Pain Perdu was created to keep the Cajuns from wasting their old bread. Thus, the name. The bread that was lost became the center of the creation. What a special treat! Now Cajuns can't wait for their bread to get stale!

COUSH-COUSH

2 cups cornmeal
$^1/_3$ cup flour, all-purpose
$1^1/_2$ tsp. salt
1 tbsp. baking powder
2 tbsp. sugar

$^1/_2$ cup lard
$1^1/_4$ cup milk
Milk and sugar as desired
Pure cane syrup as desired

In a mixing bowl, thoroughly combine the cornmeal, flour, salt, baking powder, and sugar until well mixed. Add the milk and blend well; it should be a thick, mushy mixture. In a heavy, black iron skillet, heat the lard over medium-high heat until it is hot, then add the cornmeal mixture. Let it cook over medium high heat until a crust forms, then give it a good stir to make the brown crust spread throughout the dish; reduce the heat to low. Cover and simmer for 15 minutes. Serve hot with milk and sugar as you would serve cereal, or drizzle with cane syrup, then cover with milk. Serves 4 to 6.

Lagniappe: No making in advance; just make it when you are ready to eat. A real Cajun breakfast dish or a late-night treat! I like to fry bacon to eat with my coush-coush. You can also serve the dish without mixing in the milk. Just cover it with cane syrup with a huge glass of milk on the side. This is simple food that was very filling and allowed the Cajuns to work hard throughout the day without growing hungry. It is a dish that "sticks" to you and holds you well.

Today, it's just comfort food! Coush-coush was also served with fresh milk clabber and called Coush-Coush et Caille. To make the latter, get fresh milk clabber and mix it with the Coush-Coush and add sugar or pure cane syrup. This dish is a breakfast that was handed down to the Cajuns from the area Indians of the bayous. To be quite honest, I love coush-coush, but I just can't eat it with clabber!

BLACKBERRY PRESERVES

3 qts. blackberries
Water to cover
2 qts. sugar

$^1/_2$ tsp. salt
$^1/_4$ cup fresh lemon juice
$^1/_2$ cup water

Wash and pick over the blackberries to be sure that no leaves or other pieces of the plant are mixed in. Drain the berries well, pour them into a large saucepot, and add the sugar, salt, lemon juice, and water. Place the pot over medium-high heat and bring the mixture to a hard boil; carefully stir to make sure all the sugar has dissolved and all of the berries are in their liquid. Continue to boil for 15 minutes, then reduce the heat to low and let the preserves simmer for 15 more minutes, stirring every so often. Remove from the heat and allow the berries to cool. Pour them into pint canning jars and seal the jars in a water bath. When the seal has set, remove and let the jars cool. They may be kept on a shelf until ready to use. Makes about 3 to 4 pints of preserves.

Lagniappe: First, I always like to keep one or two pints of freshly made blackberry preserves in a bowl in the refrigerator to use right away. The rest of the preserves can be set for later use during the year. Nothing was more fun as a kid than going blackberry picking when the berries were plentiful and ripe. They were sweet and tart at the same time and covered the pastures around my home when I was young.

We'd go out and pick them all day and bring home big containers loaded with the wild fruit. We couldn't wait for mom to make blackberry preserves for us to eat with toast or fresh French bread in the morning or for a late night treat. This was the use of a plentiful fresh wild fruit that provided sweets throughout the year, as we would can much of the excess for use all year round. Nothing was as good as when the preserves were first made. This is a very simple recipe, but the natural flavor of the fruit is what makes this a real treat. You can also serve the preserves on top of fresh warm pancakes in place of syrup.

You can use this same recipe to make Fig Preserves by doing the following: Soak the 3 quarts of figs in 3 quarts of water with $1/4$ cup of baking soda for 20 minutes. Drain the liquid well and place the figs into a large saucepot and cover with the 2 quarts of sugar. Add the lemon juice and water and bring to a boil. Cook for 20 minutes at a hard boil, then reduce the heat to a low simmer and let the figs cook for $2^1/_2$ hours, stirring often. Remove from the heat and allow them to cool. Pour into sterilized pint canning jars and seal in a water bath.

Both of these preserves are great treats throughout the year. As a young kid, I used to hate to pick figs. We had three large fig trees in the backyard, and my brothers and I used to take turns picking the figs. I'd always look for a way to keep from picking the figs, but I always liked to eat the finished product. Two preserves, both delicious and both easy to cook!

SEASONING MIXES. SAUCES. BREAKFAST

BEIGNETS

3½ cups flour, all-purpose,
  sifted
1 tsp. salt
¼ cup sugar
3 tbsp. shortening
½ cup boiling water
1 pkg. dry yeast

¼ cup warm water
1 cup milk
2 large eggs, well beaten
Shortening for greasing a
  mixing bowl
1 qt. cooking oil
2 cups powdered sugar

In a large mixing bowl, add the sifted flour, salt, and sugar and use a wire whisk to stir well to make sure the mixture is well blended. Add the shortening to the flour and pour the boiling water on top of the shortening to make it begin to melt. In a small mixing bowl, mix together the dry yeast and the warm ¼ cup of water until the yeast has dissolved. Then add it, the milk, and eggs to the flour bowl and, using your hands, mix until the dough begins to form and you can make the mixture into a ball. Place the ball in another mixing bowl that has all its sides greased. Cover with a damp towel, set it aside, and let the mixture double in size. That will take about 1 hour. Remove the ball from the bowl, lightly dust it with flour, wrap it in wax paper, and refrigerate for 2 hours.

When you are ready to cook, add the cooking oil to a deep-fat fryer or large, deep skillet and bring the oil to 350 degrees. While the oil is getting hot, lightly flour a surface for rolling the dough. Place the ball of dough in the middle of the floured surface and roll it to about ¼ inch thickness. Cut the dough into 2-inch triangles or rectangles. Deep fry in the hot oil until golden brown, then turn each beignet over and cook

SEASONING MIXES. SAUCES. BREAKFAST

the other side until it is a golden brown as well.

They should puff up and gain a lot of volume. Remove to a plate that is covered with paper towels. Sprinkle generously with powdered sugar while the beignets are hot. Repeat the process until all the dough is fried. Serve hot. Makes about 30 beignets.

Lagniappe: This is the early form of the donut! They are not glazed, but powdered to give them their sweetness. This is a puffed dough and is a great breakfast treat. It does take a little preparation time, but the time is well spent when this end product is obtained. When I was a kid, my grandmother used to make beignets, but she'd make them much larger, pan fry them in a very little bit of shortening, and then we'd butter them and put pure cane syrup on them.

We called them "salty donuts" because they weren't sweet, and you had to put syrup on them. I guess we were comparing them to the sweet glazed donuts at the bakery. She would sprinkle them with the powdered sugar, but we liked them better with butter and cane syrup. Whether or not you make them smaller and deep fry them or whether you make them larger and pan fry them this recipe is the same.

INDEX